The Smarter Bet™ Guide to Poker

Basil Nestor

Sterling Publishing Co., Inc.
New York

**For Flora and Pauline. Always play your best hand.
Never go on tilt. Enjoy the game.**

Acknowledgments

Thanks to Ron Luks and the rest of the members in CompuServe's Las Vegas Forum. Thanks to Fay Nestor for her loving support.

Special thanks and kudos to my editor Sharyn Rosart. Her vision and determination have made the Smarter Bet series possible. Thanks also to Lynne Yeamans for her design.

10 9 8 7 6 5 4 3 2 1

Published 2003 by Sterling Publishing Co., Inc.
387 Park Avenue South, New York, NY 10016
Previously published by the Dorset Press
© 2002 by Basil Nestor
Distributed in Canada by Sterling Publishing
c/o Canadian Manda Group, One Atlantic Avenue, Suite 105
Toronto, Ontario, Canada M6K 3E7
Distributed in Great Britain by Chrysalis Books
64 Brewery Road, London N7 9NT, England
Distributed in Australia by Capricorn Link (Australia) Pty. Ltd.
P.O. Box 704, Windsor, NSW 2756, Australia

Printed in Hong Kong
All rights reserved

Sterling ISBN 1-4027-0962-5

Contents

Introduction
America's Game

Is there any English-speaking person who hasn't heard the expressions "fold a losing hand," "read 'em and weep," "poker face," "holding all the cards," or "the buck stops here"? And consider, "You gotta know when to hold 'em, and know when to fold 'em." Who in North America is entirely unfamiliar with Kenny Rogers' musical musings about poker strategy?

Clearly, poker is more than a gambling game; it's a social phenomenon.

Poker and its ersatz versions (video poker, Caribbean Stud Poker, Let It Ride, and other poker-based games) together account for more wagering in North America than any other gambling contest. Think about it. Who plays blackjack at home? How often do the guys get together to play slots or lottery at someone's kitchen table? Poker is simply everywhere.

How did this happen? Why is the game so hard-wired into our culture?

The origins of America's love affair with poker can be traced (somewhat prophetically) to about the time Christopher Columbus stumbled onto the New World. Europe was in the middle of a Renaissance that was spreading outward from Italy. Europeans were reading, talking, experimenting, looking into the heavens, creating new art, and doing all sorts of radical and exciting things that inevitably made the feudal lords and other bastions of the establishment very unhappy. One of the basic shifts in thinking involved the value of the individual versus society. Upward mobility began challenging the class system. Winning was okay again.

The earliest forms of blackjack and lotto developed around this time, as well as a contest known as primero.

Each primero player received four cards. A player could bid, stake, or pass. The object was to lure weaker opponents into betting and then beat them with a stronger hand, thus winning the pot (all of the accumulated bets). The top hand was "chorus," four-of-a-kind, and the next-strongest hand was "fluxus," four cards of the same suit. It's not hard to imagine an exuberant player showing fluxus and reaching for the pot. Suddenly, his opponent would reveal chorus and speak the old Italian equivalent of "not so fast, pardner."

Primero followed the outward wave of the Renaissance over the next few hundred years and morphed into games like *gilet*, *brelan*, and *bouillotte* in France, and *gleek*, *post and pair*, and *bragg* in England. All the contests shared the same beguiling characteristics: every player had an equal probability of being dealt the best hand, they all bet into a pot, and winners used strategy to lure weaker opponents into losing situations.

Charles Cotton, a seventeenth-century writer, gave this description of gleek in 1674: "The first or eldest says, 'I'll vie the Ruff,' the next says, 'I'll see it,' and the third, 'I'll see it and revie it.'" Cotton went on to report, "Sometimes out of policy or a vapour they will vie when they have not above thirty in their hands, and the rest may have forty or fifty, and being afraid to see it, the first many times wins out of meer bravado."

It was a bluff! Doesn't that bring a tear to your eye?

A German version of this game was called *poquen*. The original word was *pochspiel*, which meant "to defy" or "push". The French changed *poquen* to *poque*, and that's the contest that appeared in New Orleans at the beginning of the nineteenth century. It was similar to the Persian game *as-nas*, and some scholars trace poker through Persia (modern-day Iran) mostly because *as-nas* has five-card hands. It was *poque*, *as-nas*, or some derivation of those two games that Joseph Cowell saw on a Mississippi riverboat in 1829. Cowell was an English actor touring the United States, and he wrote a colorful account of a game dealt by "Green Spectacles," a riverboat card-cheat whose plans went awry. The "blackleg" stacked the deck, but then accidentally misdealt and gave the best cards, four aces and a king, to one of his opponents. Green Spectacles took the defeat in stride (and preserved his health) by pushing the enormous $2,023 pot away with a sigh while saying, "Did you ever see the like on't?"

Interestingly, Cowell wasn't as horrified about the cheating as he was impressed with the atmosphere and experience surrounding the game. According to the Englishman, "Jack was as good as his master, and never was Republicanism more practically republicanized."

Like all things imported and then enthusiastically adopted by America, the name of the game was promptly mangled. It changed from *poque* to poker as it traveled up the Mississippi and went west with the settlers. The earliest rules were five cards face-down with no draw. Pairs, three-of-a-kind, and four-of-a-kind were the goal. The concepts of draw, flush, and straight (see Chapter 1) didn't come along until mid-century. Stud (cards dealt face up) was invented during the Civil War, but Wild Bill Hickok played draw poker. That was the game of choice in the Old West. The image of gunslingers sitting around a table with each man holding five cards has since been indelibly etched into the minds of Americans via countless movies, books, and songs. To this day, novice poker players are stunned when they walk into a modern poker room and find nobody playing draw poker.

At about the time that Wild Bill Hickok was sitting down for his last game (he was shot in the back while holding aces and eights), the U.S. ambassador to England, Robert C. Schenck, was writing one of the first comprehensive guides to the rules of the contest. The English were enchanted with poker, and it was popular in the court of Queen Victoria.

Poker inspired the invention of the slot machine at the turn of the century (the earliest slot machines were poker machines), and the game paradoxically flourished as the temperance movement gathered strength and legal gambling venues were closed. Poker was never an ideal casino game because it didn't have a built-in advantage for the house, but this characteristic made it the perfect game for people who wanted to gamble in small private groups. Who needed a casino? Ironically, the temperance movement permanently welded poker into the national lifestyle.

Consider this amazing linguistic metamorphosis: Poker's rotating dealer was often designated by a buckhorn knife in frontier days. The knife was replaced by a silver dollar as the frontier gave way to towns, and so dollars came to be called "bucks." When players passed the responsibility of dealing to someone else they were "passing the buck." One young man from Missouri who loved the game later became president of the United States. That man, Harry Truman, immortalized the phrase, "The buck stops here." Three universal metaphors from just one tiny function.

That's the power of poker. The whole game is a reflection of American life, and vice versa.

Sit down at any poker table and the verbal descriptions become even more vivid. One player is "hiding in the blind." Another is "under the gun," but he has top pair and hopes to "make it to the river." Someone is "chasing," intending to "run him down at the turn." The challenger is on a "gutshot straight draw." A ten falls, and the former challenger is "holding the nuts" (an unbeatable combination). Top pair is "drawing dead."

That's the colorful language of the frontier, still wonderfully alive in poker.

These days poker is more popular than ever. The dominant versions are hold 'em and seven-card stud, though dozens of other variations flourish. People play poker around the world. Tens of thousands of poker machines merrily beep and ring in countless casinos (though purists claim this isn't really poker). Hundred of small tournaments are played every week throughout the nation, and there's a big-money tournament circuit with the crown jewel at the World Series of Poker in Las Vegas. Top prize last year was $1.5 million. In the true spirit of poker, anyone willing to pay the $10,000 entry fee is welcome to compete.

Who knows? Someday you might go all the way at the World Series of Poker. But to do that you have to learn how to inexpensively fold a fluxus (flush) when someone else is holding a chorus (four of a kind).

That's what this book is about, so let's get started.

Part 1

A
♠

Basic Concepts

Chapter 1

Poker Fundamentals

IMAGINE IF YOU COULD PAY A PENNY AND BUY JUST THE FIRST two numbers on a lottery ticket. If those numbers hit, then you could buy a few additional numbers for a nickel. Finally, just before the last number came up, you could discard the ticket or pay full price. Wouldn't that be an amazing advantage?

That's how poker works.

We'll explore the lottery analogy more in later chapters, but right now just remember that a "preview" system exists in poker, and many players don't quite realize it. Some do, but they have an incomplete understanding of how it works. Only a small percentage of players fully comprehend this system and all its ramifications.

This uneven distribution of knowledge is a powerful factor in the game. Poker players have widely varying levels of competence (or incompetence). In fact, poker has more in common with golf than it does with most gambling games.

Yes, it sounds strange, but it's true. For example, most gambling contests put players on one side, and the casino (or state) is on the other side. Professionals can squeeze out a positive edge in some situations, but in most contests the house has an absolute advantage. That's why there are no gambling professionals who earn a living playing roulette, slots, keno, or craps. It's not mathematically possible to win at those games in the long run.

Luck vs. Skill

There are a few professionals who earn a living playing blackjack, and even fewer who sustain themselves playing video poker, but it's tough. Perfect play will produce about a one-percent player edge. Skill is important in those contests, but luck still holds a tremendous sway.

It's the other way around in poker. Luck has an influence, but skill has a more pronounced effect. The opponent isn't a monolithic casino with a built-in advantage. Instead, it's a wide range of people with varying levels of expertise. A few are full-time professionals earning a steady living. Some are semi-professionals who supplement their regular income with poker winnings. Most are casual players with average to marginal skill who enjoy the game and play once a week or a few times a year. Doesn't that sound like golf?

Poker even has a tournament circuit. Pros make the rounds to earn their living. There are big-money events and smaller contests. Beginners often compete with champions, just as in a golf pro-am.

Understanding the similarities between poker and golf and the fundamental differences between poker and most casino contests is important for a number of reasons. First, your money is potentially at *greater* risk when playing poker than it is when playing typical gambling games. The **house edge** (built-in casino advantage) slowly bleeds you dry in most gambling contests, but it protects you as well. The mathematics are set. Sometimes you win and more times they win. Not so in poker. If you're a beginner or someone who relies mostly on luck, and you unwittingly play against someone who has superior skill, it's like playing eighteen holes against Tiger Woods. You'll lose.

Another result of this situation is that all players, even people at lower-stakes tables, will sometimes find themselves sitting across from professionals or semi-professionals. Pros don't look like movie villains. They don't wear signs or black hats. They act like everyone else, your buddies, your neighbors. But pros take your money.

The sweet lady with a beehive hairdo, the kindly old man with caramels in his pocket, the young guy in a wheelchair, the cute girl with a ponytail…will suck the Andy Jacksons straight out of your wallet.

Would you like to reverse that flow and become a consistent winner? It takes more than just learning the rules of poker. You must be willing to go beyond luck and acquire skill. You must be willing to defeat your opponents.

There's nothing mean-spirited or antisocial about it. It's an honest competition with many challengers, but only one winner. That's the same fundamental hurdle facing competitors in any sport. Yes, serendipity plays a role, but strategy and discipline are ultimately more powerful than the capricious whims of coincidence. There is lucky and there is good. Luck eventually turns. Good is forever. See? Poker is like golf.

And remember, you don't have to be the Tiger Woods of poker to be a consistent winner. You just have to be better than the other people at the table. One of the nice things about poker is that (to some degree) you can choose your opponents.

The Way It Really Is

It's a typical scene from movies and television. Four or five peo-ple sit at a round table. A single bright light shines from above. The year is 1880 or maybe 1920. Each person holds five cards. The bad guy throws some cash into the pot and says, "I'll see your $800 (dramatic pause) and raise you $3,000." Then he tosses another stack of bills onto the pile. The hero must fold or bet the farm.

Modern casino poker is hardly like that, so forget the media images. Also, set aside most of what you learned about poker when playing at home (unless you only intend to challenge grandpa for quarters). Home-style **five-card draw** and games with **wild cards** are rarely seen in casinos.

The two most popular poker versions are **Texas hold 'em** (often just called hold 'em) and **seven-card stud**. Other common versions include **Omaha hi/lo**, and **pineapple**. All are played with a standard 52-card deck. We'll cover these versions and a few more later. Right now we're going to focus on the common ele-ments of every genuine poker contest.

Players, Pot, and Showdown

All genuine poker games have multiple players, typically six to nine people, competing to win a single **pot** (the combined bets of all the players). The pile of money increases as cards are dealt and players with strong poker hands (or bluffers representing strong hands) bet into the pot. Other players must match the bets or give up, thus losing whatever money they have invested. The contest ends when everyone concedes to one player, or when two or more players match bets in the final round and there is a **showdown**. The remaining players reveal their hands and compare them. The person with the best poker hand wins the pot.

Note that poker-based contests such as video poker, Caribbean Stud Poker, Let It Ride, Three Card Poker, pai gow poker, and many other recently developed games don't have all three of these basic poker elements (multiple players, a pot, and a showdown). Quasi-poker games are certainly fun to play, but they're closer in function to craps and blackjack than traditional poker, so we don't cover them in this book.

If you're looking for video poker strategies, check out the *Smarter Bet Guide to Slots and Video Poker*.

"If you can't spot the sucker in your first half-hour at the table, then you're the sucker."
—Mike McDermott (played by Matt Damon) in *Rounders*

Ranking the Hands

Poker hands are ranked in winning order as follows:

ROYAL FLUSH: Ace, king, queen, jack, and ten of the same suit. A royal flush can be made four different ways, but you'll be lucky if you see one in a lifetime.

STRAIGHT FLUSH: Five cards of the same suit in exactly adjacent ranks. Another example would be 5♠ 4♠ 3♠ 2♠ A♠. Note that an ace is used to make the lowest straight flush.

FOUR OF A KIND: Four cards of the same rank and a fifth card of any rank and suit.

FULL HOUSE: Three cards of the same rank and a pair of another rank.

FLUSH: Five cards of the same suit that are not exactly adjacent ranks.

STRAIGHT: Five cards not of the same suit in exactly adjacent ranks. An ace is used to make both the highest and the lowest straight.

THREE OF A KIND: Three cards of the same rank and two cards of different ranks.

TWO PAIRS: Two cards of one rank, two cards of another rank, and a fifth card of a third rank.

ONE PAIR: Two cards of one rank and three cards of different ranks.

NO PAIR: Five cards that don't make any combination.

Exactly five cards are used to determine a winner, no less and no more. Even though a five-card hand may be built from seven or more cards (depending on the game), those extra cards don't count in a showdown.

When two or more hands of the same rank (two straights, two flushes, etc) are in a showdown, the high cards in each hand determine the winner. For example, a queen-high straight flush beats a jack-high straight flush. Three kings beat three jacks. A pair of aces beat a pair of queens. An ace-high flush beats a flush that has a high card of ten. If both players have identical combinations (both have two kings and two aces), then the highest non-paired card in the hand determines the winner. This lone card is known as a kicker.

Full houses are judged first by the three matching cards and then by the pair, so kings full of jacks (three kings and two jacks) beats queens full of aces.

If neither hand makes a pair, then the hand with the highest card wins. If that card is matched, then the next card is used to decide, and so on. The pot is split when all five cards match in rank. Suit is never used to determine a winner. The order of the cards has no importance.

What are the chances that your **trips** (three of a kind) will be beaten by a straight? The following table shows the total number of possible five-card combinations that can be dealt from a 52-card deck. The column on the far right shows the probability of receiving any particular hand when exactly five cards are dealt.

Remember, the probability of making a hand changes as the cards are

Smarter Bet Factoid

Some versions of poker are played for low, meaning that the worst hand wins. It sounds easy, but it's tougher than you might think. You have an equal probability of being dealt the best hand or the worst hand. For more on low hands, see Chapter 8.

Frequency of Poker Hands

Hand	Number of Occurrences	Percent Probability
Royal Flush	4	0.00015%
Straight Flush	36	0.0014%
Four-of-a-kind	624	0.02%
Full House	3,744	0.14%
Flush	5,108	0.20%
Straight	10,200	0.39%
Three-of-a-kind	54,912	2.11%
Two Pair	123,552	4.75%
One Pair	1,098,240	42.26%
Everything Else	1,302,540	50.12%
Total	**2,598,960**	

The column on the far right shows the probability of receiving any particular hand when exactly five cards are dealt. It's somewhat easier to make a hand with seven cards (as in seven-card stud or hold 'em), but less than 39% of seven-card hands are two pairs or better.

revealed. For example, if you already have four cards to a flush, then the chance of finishing with a flush is significantly higher. And it's easier to make a hand when using more than five cards (as in hold 'em and seven-card stud). Nevertheless, you may go a lifetime without seeing a "natural" royal flush.

The Object of the Game

It is a curious fact that players with the strongest hands often win the smallest pots. And players who win the most pots usually lose the most money.

I'll explain why as we go along, but right now just remember that the ultimate goal in poker is not to have a superior hand or to win a lot of pots.

The goal in poker is to win the most money.

Everything we cover, every element of the game (including the importance of following the rules and playing with integrity), every decision you make, every moment at the table is entirely about this one purpose. Never let yourself be distracted by any other poker goals; beating your opponent, exposing a bluff, winning a long-shot, or stacking a big pile of chips can all be tremendous fun, but they won't necessarily make you a poker winner.

Of course, having fun is important. Life is too short to have a bad time, but if you allow the pursuit of pleasure to supersede profit in poker then you'll be a pleasure-seeking loser. Players in this mindset are referred to as **live ones**, and they are beloved and welcome in any poker gathering (most especially mine). They prefer mindless risk to reward. A heart-thumping challenge is the only thing that turns them on. Winning pots is their goal; winning the most money is entirely a secondary concern.

Live ones come in two types. There are jovial ones who know they're at a disadvantage; they play for recreation with the expectation of losing. The other type are complainers; they blame their losses on bad luck, a bad seat, the deck, the dealer, the poker gods, anything but their own poor play.

Keep in mind that live ones (even complainers) are not nec-essarily unpleasant people. In fact, they're great to have around. Believe me, it's a tremendous ego boost when people constantly call you "lucky."

And that creates an interesting irony. Players who depend primarily on luck usually don't see it too often. But players who study the game and play well seem to have plenty of good luck and also a lot more fun. Poker is a lot like life.

In Review

A♥ **Poker is different** from most gambling games because the opponent in poker is not a casino; the opponents are other players who have various skill levels.

2♥ **Casino poker games** are typically played with a 52-card deck (no wild cards).

3♥ **Poker hand rankings** reflect the probability that a particular hand will appear in a randomly dealt five-card combination. Higher hands occur less frequently.

4♥ **The object in poker** is to win the most money. Winning the most pots or having the best hand is not necessarily the best way to win the most money.

Chapter 2

2 ♦

Playing Casino Poker

ONE OF THE NICE THINGS ABOUT POKER IS THAT YOU CAN play it almost anywhere. That's how it became America's favorite gambling game.

Game venues typically fall into three categories: private gatherings of friends and family, private gatherings of acquaintances and strangers, and public settings (casinos and card rooms).

One might assume that the rules of poker and the strategies for winning would be the same no matter where the game might be played (and indeed, in a perfect world that would be true). But practically speaking, venue has a powerful influence on the nature of the contest.

Casino Poker vs. Private Poker

Playing poker at home with friends or family can be tremendous fun, but the standards of competition and the potential for profit are generally pretty low. You're understandably less eager to play well and win $1,000 from your dad. Also, private games of this type are usually "loosey-goosey." Rules are bent to soothe feelings. Winners feel obligated to play longer and give losers a chance to get even. It's all very healthy in the context of a tight-knit group, but it's not usually high-quality poker.

The next step up is private gatherings of acquaintances and strangers. These are more formal and the potential for profit is greater, but rules are still occasionally bent. There's no real authority to settle disputes, and cheating is a real possibility. Games like this are often the grist for crime novels and movie scripts. These venues dominated the world of poker through much of the last century. They still exist, but they've been replaced mostly by public poker.

These days, casinos and card rooms are the premier venues for quality poker. They're open all day, every day of the year. There's no need to organize a game or wait for Thursday night. You can win as much as you want without guilt, leave the table when you're ready to stop, or play as long as you like when everyone else wants to quit; new players will be waiting to join the game. Rules are equitably enforced. Security guards patrol the casino and the parking lot. You don't even need to bring cash; there's an ATM machine just a few steps away.

Best of all, you don't need to be Bat Masterson or Calamity Jane to play and win in a public venue. You simply need good strategy and a clear head.

Choosing a Game and Buying In

Not every casino has poker, but if one does, it's usually in a space set apart from the hubbub of slots and other games. Some casinos (often called card clubs) primarily offer poker, and in these situations it's the hubbub that is set apart while poker dominates the layout.

Either way, you'll find a reception desk at or near the entrance to the poker area. A host there will be organizing games. If a seat is not immediately available, the host will put your name on a list and call you when something opens up. Games are identified by the type of poker (seven-card stud, hold 'em, etc.) and by betting limits, 3-6, 6-12, 20-40, or some other combination of numbers. In a **fixed-limit** game the first number is the dollar amount that can be bet or raised in the early rounds (usually round one and two); the second number is the amount that can be bet or raised in later rounds. A **spread-limit** game allows any bet between two amounts at any time. **No-limit** means just what it says; any amount can be bet at any time (very dangerous for beginners). **Pot-limit** means any amount up to the current value of the pot can be bet at any time. The strategy examples in this book apply to fixed-limit games unless otherwise stated.

The first order of business once you're seated will be to exchange cash for chips. This is called a **buy-in**. Put your money on the table, and the dealer or a chip-person will handle the transaction.

Most games have a minimum required buy-in that is usually about five times the maximum bet of that particular game ($40 for a 4-8 game). You're better off buying in for at least three to five times that amount. I'll explain why in a later section.

Smarter Bet Tip

You should stick to low-limit games until you're an experienced player. Start with 2-4, 3-6, or 4-8. Don't go above 6-12 until you're entirely satisfied with your performance at the lower limits.

A typical poker table has seven to nine players. That's you and a bunch of strangers who want your money. Get ready to swim with the sharks.

Seven-Card Stud and Texas Hold 'Em

Seven-card stud is one of the oldest forms of poker, and it was the most-played poker version through much of the twentieth century. It's still found everywhere (especially in the northeastern U.S.), but in the last few decades new games have emerged that have challenged seven-card stud's dominance.

As a group these new contests are called **flop games**. The most popular is Texas hold 'em. Others are Omaha hi/lo, and pineapple.

Part of the reason for the growing dominance of flop games (particularly hold 'em) is that they're faster and somewhat easier to play than seven-card stud, yet they're no less responsive to strategy. Also, Texas hold 'em is the game that determines the world champion in the annual World Series of Poker.

All of these factors make hold 'em an ideal "learning" version. So this book begins with hold 'em and expands to seven-card stud in a later section.

But remember, many of the strategies in the hold 'em chapters (especially those in Chapter 5) apply to all genuine poker contests. You'll be four-fifths of the way to knowing every poker version on earth by the time we cover seven-card stud.

Community Cards

Each player receives only two cards in Texas hold 'em. They are face down. During the course of play, five additional cards are dealt face up on the **board** (the table) as **community cards**; these are shared by all the players. We'll cover betting and raising in a later section; for right now just remember that players use the community cards and their two **pocket cards** or **hole cards** to build a five-card poker hand. A final hand can include one, both, or in some circumstances none of the pocket cards.

Yes, it's very different from the games you've seen in the movies, but this is how poker is played around the world.

"I'd equate it with chess or other games of skill that require multilevel strategic, mathematical, or psychological skills. For the people who play it seriously, there's no luck involved at all."

—Edward Norton, on his role in *Rounders*

Let's say you have: Your opponent has:

And the board shows:

You have an ace-high flush A♠ J♠ 10♠ 8♠ 2♠, and your opponent has a king-high straight K♥ Q♦ J♦ 10♠ 9♦. You would win this hand in a showdown. If you hold:

Your opponent has:

And the board shows:

You have a full house, kings full of aces, but your opponent has a higher full house, aces full of kings.

Here is a **bad beat** example from a hand I once played.

I was holding:

My opponent was holding:

The board was:

My ace-high flush was beaten by a jack-high straight flush, and my opponent used only one card from his hand to do it.

The concept of community cards may seem odd at first, but as you can see it's a strong advantage for experienced players because reading your opponents' hands is much easier in an **open game** (some cards dealt face up) than in a **closed game** (no cards revealed) like five-card draw.

For example, a full house is not possible in hold 'em unless there is a pair on the board. A flush is not possible unless the board has at least three suited cards. A straight is not possible unless three cards are within five ranks of each other.

Holding the Nuts

The straight flush in the previous section is an unbeatable hand. In other words, a higher hand is not possible with that particular combination of cards on the board. A person who holds an unbeatable combination is said to be holding the **nuts**.

Recognizing when you have the nuts (or when you don't) is an important part of profitable poker. Going back through the examples, the nuts for A♥ K♣ 5♠ A♠ 9♥ are AA unless you're holding one ace, in which case the nuts are AK (making a full house). No higher hand is possible.

For Q♦ 10♠ 2♠ J♦ 8♠, the nuts are an ace of spades and any other spade. The ace creates a **nut flush**, a flush that cannot be beaten. A straight made with an ace or two high cards would be a nut straight.

Betting, Raising, and Folding

You're probably familiar with the concept of an **ante**. It's a small bet made by all the players in a hand to start the pot. This puts money in play and it makes additional bets worth the risk.

Five-card draw and seven-card stud use antes, but hold 'em doesn't. Instead it uses a rotating system of **blind bets** to start the pot. Each player is designated in turn as **dealer** for one hand. This doesn't mean the person handles the deck, but it does mean a disk called a **button** or **puck** is put in front of the player. The two players to the left of the designated dealer must make blind bets to start the pot. The first player to the left of the button makes a **small blind bet** that is less than the table minimum. The exact amount varies depending on the game and the casino. The second player makes a **big blind bet** that is usually the table minimum. Some games have just one blind.

The casino dealer will confirm that the blinds have been **posted** (placed on the table), then she'll shuffle the cards and begin the hand.

Cards are dealt clockwise starting to the left of the button. Each player receives two cards that are face down. Players carefully lift the cards, look at them, then put them back on the table. There are rules for handling cards that we'll cover in the next chapter, but the important thing to remember here is that you'll generally look at the cards once, and they'll remain face down through the rest of the hand.

The first action (opportunity to act) begins with the person to the left of the big blind. That player has three options:

FOLD: This is an unconditional surrender. The player returns her cards to the dealer and is out of the hand.

CALL: Match the previous bet (in this case it's the bet posted by the big blind). This allows the player to stay in the game and continue playing for the pot.

RAISE: Match the previous bet and then bet exactly that much more (in a fixed-limit contest). This allows the player to remain in the game and requires everyone else to call the increased amount, raise, or fold.

A fourth option is sometimes used on later rounds.

CHECK: Neither bet nor fold. The action passes to the next player. This option is available only when a bet has not yet been made in that round. Players who check and then raise a subsequent bet have performed a **check-raise**. It's an aggressive move that is prohibited in some private games, but is generally allowed in casinos.

Smarter Bet Tip

Action in the first round of hold 'em always begins with the first player to the left of the big blind, and it proceeds clockwise until all the players have called or folded to a single player. In later rounds, action always begins with the first active player to the left of the button.

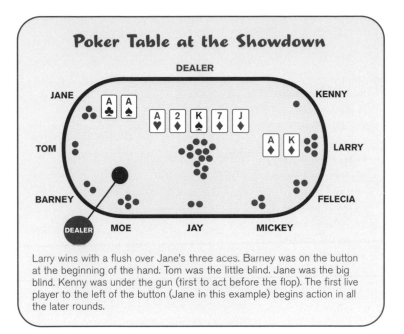

Poker Table at the Showdown

Larry wins with a flush over Jane's three aces. Barney was on the button at the beginning of the hand. Tom was the little blind. Jane was the big blind. Kenny was under the gun (first to act before the flop). The first live player to the left of the button (Jane in this example) begins action in all the later rounds.

Anatomy of a Poker Hand

Now let's put it all together. Here's an example of how a hand in a 3-6 game might develop.

BEFORE THE FLOP

Kenny is **under the gun**; he is sitting to the left of the big blind, and he's the first player to act. Kenny calls the big blind with a bet of $3. Larry is on Kenny's left; he raises $3 for a total wager

Smarter Bet Factoid

If players call the big blind, but none of them raise, then the big blind can check and end the first round of betting or "raise herself" when the action comes around.

of $6. Felecia (to the left of Larry) must either call the $6 wager, fold, or raise another $3 to make it $9. Felecia raises. The other players must either put in $9, fold, or raise again.

Four players fold after Felecia and the action moves to Tom, the little blind, who is to the left of the button. He's already got $2 in the pot. So he must put in an additional $7, fold, or raise. He folds.

Jane is the big blind. She raises another $3 for a total bet of $12. This particular table has a **cap** of three raises per round so everyone remaining in the hand must either call $12 or fold. No more raises are allowed.

The action moves back to Kenny, the original caller. He decides that his hand was worth $3 but not $12, and he folds. Larry and Felecia call. The pot is now $41.

THE FLOP

After everyone has either called or folded, the dealer **burns** the top card from the deck (removes that card from play without revealing it). This is a standard security measure to prevent cheating.

The next three cards in the deck are dealt face up on the table. This is known as the **flop**. The board shows:

The first active player to the left of the button starts the betting in this round and in every subsequent round.

That would be Jane in this example. She checks. Larry bets $3. Felecia folds. Jane raises Larry $3 (a check-raise). Ouch! Larry now wonders if Jane is suckering him or bluffing. Larry is holding:

That gives him two pairs (aces and kings). There are only three possible hands that Jane could be holding to beat Larry at this point. AA, KK, or 22 would give her three of a kind. Larry calls, "Time." This is a verbal declaration requesting a pause in the action.

Larry thinks it over. Perhaps Jane is holding a combination that he can currently beat or tie (AK, AQ, AJ, etc). He decides to test her hand with a reraise. Larry puts another $6 in the pot (matching Jane's $3 raise and adding an extra $3).

Jane raises again. Larry decides she has a **set** (trips made with a pocket pair), or she's got nerves of steel. He calls. The total in the pot is now $65.

THE TURN AND THE RIVER

The dealer burns another card and a fourth card is revealed. This round is known as the **turn**. Betting levels are double the previous rounds.

The turn card is 7♦. Larry still has two pairs, but now he also has four cards to a diamond flush. Once again, Jane is first to act because she is the first player to the left of the button. This time she doesn't check. She bets $6. Larry calls. The pot swells to $77.

40

Another burned card, and the last card is revealed. It's a J♦. This round is called the **river**. The board shows:

| A ♥ | 2 ♦ | K ♠ | 7 ♦ | J ♦ |

Remember that Larry is holding A♦ K♦, so his hand has improved to an ace-high diamond flush. There is no pair on the board, and that means a full house is not possible. Ditto for a straight flush or royal flush. Larry has the nuts. Jane checks. Larry bets $6. Jane calls. The betting is concluded. The dealer asks both players to reveal their hands for the showdown. Larry flips up his ace and king. Jane turns over A♣ A♠. She was winning with trips until the last card. The dealer pushes $89 in chips to Larry, moves the button clockwise to the next player, and the new hand begins.

Larry's profit was $53 ($89 less his contribution of $36). Jane lost $36. Felecia lost $12. Kenny lost $3. Tom lost $2. The other players folded before contributing anything to the pot.

ANALYSIS OF THE ACTION

That's the kind of showdown that gets your heart thumping. Stacking the chips makes you feel ten feet tall, and being the loser makes you wonder if the poker gods hate you. But Larry and Jane are both good players. They'll think about the hand before taking credit or assigning blame.

Here's the beautiful part. Both of them will conclude that they played their hands properly (which they both did). In fact, the person who made the mistake was Kenny. He either called with a weak hand, or improperly threw away a strong one. Of course, he lost only $3, but it's the little leaks that eventually sink the battleship bankroll. Also, Kenny revealed information about his lack of expertise. Larry and Jane will use that profitably.

Now you might be saying, "Wait a second. Felecia raised and then folded. She lost four times as much as Kenny. Didn't she make a mistake?"

Nope. She played her hand perfectly. I'll explain why in Part 2, but for now just assume that her strategy was correct, and consider the following scenario.

Imagine that you own a casino. When would be the best time to "quit while you're ahead?" Of course, the answer is never. A casino has an advantage. The longer it plays, the more money it earns. The same is true of poker. Setting arbitrary dollar limits (up or down) is pointless. You should play when you have an advantage, and you should fold or leave the table when you're at disadvantage. Winning or losing a particular hand means nothing. Luck happens.

Yes, you should budget your money, but a bankroll can't tell you when to bet. A "bad night" or a "good night" will not affect how the cards will fall on the next hand. Forget luck, and forget the short-term. Look to the long-term and play correctly.

In Review

A♦ **Poker games are identified by** the game type, the dollar-amount betting limits, and the betting structure (fixed-limit, spread-limit, pot-limit, or no limit).

2♦ **Hold 'em and seven-card stud** are the most popular casino poker versions. Other well-known versions such as Omaha hi/lo and pineapple are based on hold 'em.

3♦ **Hold 'em players** use two personal cards and five shared community cards to build a five-card poker hand. The game has four rounds: pre-flop, flop, turn, and river.

4♦ **If a bet has not yet been made**, players have two options when action reaches them; they can check or bet. If a bet has been made, then a player can fold, call, or raise.

5♦ **A player who holds an unbeatable hand** is said to be holding "the nuts." Recognizing when you have the nuts (or when you don't) is an important part of profitable poker.

Chapter 3

3
♥

Rules and Customs

POKER IS LIKE ANY ORGANIZED ACTIVITY; IT WORKS BEST when everyone follows the rules. Sloppy play causes confusion and delays. It can change the outcome of hands, and it generally makes a table less profitable. That's why every poker player has a responsibility to uphold and maintain the integrity of the game.

Thankfully, it's not a chore. In fact, the game is much more exciting and fast-paced when everyone follows correct procedures. Strategy is easier to apply, action is easier to track, and there is no question about who is entitled to a particular win. The worst poker catastrophe is losing a pot, or having a strong hand fouled, because someone broke the rules.

How to Handle Cards

It's bad form to lift cards completely off the table, and it's entirely against the rules to remove them from the table or conceal them in any way.

Here's one good way to look at your cards: Square them. Hold your hands over one end of the stack and use one thumb to gently squeeze up the index corners.

Put a short stack of chips on the cards when you're finished. This prevents a dealer from accidentally **mucking** your hand (retrieving the cards and tossing them into the discard pile). It happens more often than you might think. Unprotected cards are permanently dead when they hit the muck (even if the dealer made a mistake). Remember, it's your responsibility to **protect your hand** and prevent it from being **fouled** (made invalid).

There are other ways that a hand can be fouled: when two hands touch or are otherwise intermingled, when cards fall off the table, and when a player accidentally mucks cards.

Smarter Bet Tip

It's perfectly okay to look at your cards more than once, but handling them too much has some drawbacks. You may inadvertently foul your hand, and frequent glances can sometimes help your opponents guess what you're holding.

Let's say you're in a four-way showdown and an opponent announces that she has a straight. You muck a pair of aces. Another player mucks. A third player turns over a pair of kings. The last player proudly turns up a worthless hand that at first glance looks like a straight. The dealer stares at the two hands for a long moment and then announces that the kings win. The owner of the busted straight is surprised, and then realizes that she misread her hand.

Yes, it was an honest mistake, but it's too late. You mucked the aces, and your hand is dead. The pot goes to the pair of kings.

The Cards Speak

The previous scenario is the perfect reason why it's a bad idea to muck a hand in a showdown unless you're absolutely sure it's a loser. If you have any possibility of winning, it's better to expose the cards and allow the dealer to determine the winner (with the table's supervision). The rule is that **the cards speak**. In other words, verbal announcements are invalid and unnecessary; the only thing that matters is what can be seen on the cards.

Some people don't like to reveal losing hands in a show-down. They're embarrassed or they don't want to give away information about the hand they played, so they just muck. That's acceptable if a hand is clearly busted (a worthless four-flush), but I've seen many hands where the supposed winner wasn't. Here's a typical example in hold 'em:

You hold:

Your opponent has:

And the board shows:

At the showdown your opponent triumphantly flips over his hand and exclaims, "I've got the high two pair."

Does that beat a pair of jacks? Yes, it does. Should you muck? No, because your hand isn't a pair. It's two pairs: jacks and fours. You're the winner.

So when the showdown comes, don't be coy, and don't hesitate. Just reveal your cards. Announce the hand if it pleases you, but the cards speak.

Smarter Bet Factoid

Players are not required to reveal their hands if everyone folds to one player before a showdown. But if anyone mucks at a showdown, any player at the table can request to see the mucked hand. The purpose of this rule is to prevent collusion, but it should be invoked sparingly because it may offend some opponents.

It's somewhat ironic that nearly every classic betting maneuver you've seen in the movies is forbidden in real poker.

SPLASHING THE POT

Throwing chips into the pot is called **splashing the pot**. This is forbidden because the dealer and other players must be able to verify that a bettor has contributed the correct amount. The dealer must **count down** the chips in the pot if it has been splashed. This is time-consuming and a real drag. The correct way to bet is to place chips in front of your position. The dealer will collect the chips at the end of the betting round and put them in the pot.

STRING BETS

Remember the movie scene that I described in Chapter 1? "I'll see your $800 (dramatic pause) and raise you $3,000." That's called a **string bet** or **string raise**, and it's forbidden. When a player says "call," then that's it. No raise is allowed. This rule prevents a bettor from using a call as a psychological ploy to read an opponent's reaction, then morphing the call into a raise when weakness is perceived.

Another form of string bet is to say nothing, put enough chips out for a call, and then return to the stack to raise. Once again, this is forbidden. Some people do it innocently because they're just counting chips, but it's still against the rules. If an opponent objects, the wager will be restricted to a call.

The best way to avoid any confusion is to simply say, "raise." That's binding, then you can take as much time as is required to get the chips off your stack.

ACTING OUT OF TURN

Consider the hand I described in Chapter 2, when Larry won over Jane. What would have happened before the flop if Felecia had announced out of turn, "I'm raising this one"? It's probable that Kenny would have folded, and the betting might not have been capped. That would have cost Larry $3 and possibly more.

Acting out of turn is unfair, and it disrupts the game. Players should always wait until the action reaches them before tossing cards, checking, raising, or calling.

SHARING HANDS AND REVEALING CARDS

It's against the rules for someone with a live hand to reveal those cards to another active player (unless everyone else has folded).

Anyone who does this is cheating.

Some players bend this rule by showing cards to people behind them or to others who have folded at the table. Revealing cards in this manner is borderline bad form, but it's acceptable as long as the other person doesn't comment or offer advice. To do so violates the principle of **one player to a hand**. If the cards are revealed to anyone who has folded, then you have the right to see those cards when the hand is over. That rule is called **show one, show all** and it insures that everyone has equal access to the same game information.

In some sloppy games (often at lower limits), you'll hear players loudly speculating on other people's hands. "Uh oh! A pair is on the board. Hal's got a full house." This is against the rules, and you have the right to stop such comments by appealing to the dealer or a **floorperson** (casino supervisor). Ditto for people who talk about hands that they've folded.

Of course, you may profit more in some situations by saying nothing and allowing minor infractions to pass. It's a judgment call with many variables. Forcing the situation with a strict interpretation of the rules may put an opponent on guard and make him play better. You don't want that.

TAPPING THE TABLE WHILE THINKING

There are two ways to check; a player can say, "check," or he can tap the table. A person who unconsciously taps the table while thinking may be restricted to a check if other players subsequently take action. At the very least, idle tapping often causes unpleasant confusion. Other players bet or check, the thinker usually doesn't notice at first, and then he finally complains when it's too late. The whole thing can quickly become a comedy of errors.

PULLING THE POT

You've seen it in the movies. The winner reaches out and rakes in the dough. In real life you must wait for the dealer to push you the chips.

Smarter Bet Tip

If you don't have the proper denomination chip for a particular bet or raise, just state your intention and put out a larger chip (or chips). The dealer will make the appropriate change. If you don't make a verbal declaration, a larger chip will usually be considered a call unless it's closer to or exactly the denomination of a raise.

Table Stakes

When I was a youngster I would watch poker movies and think about strategy. Back then it seemed pretty straightforward; the person with the most money would simply bet more than opponents could afford to call. Competitors would thus be forced out of the pot. I promised myself to always sit down at a poker table with one million dollars, and that would insure my income forever. I never did figure out why anyone other than a millionaire would sit in a game like that, and it never occurred to me that someone with ten million might wipe me out.

In the real world of poker one cannot be forced out of the pot by running out of money. The game uses a system called **table stakes** to prevent that from happening. The chips sitting in front of a player at the beginning of a hand are the only ones that can be used in the hand. If a player runs out of chips, this is called being **all in**. A **side pot** is created from subsequent bets and raises. The player who is all in can win the main pot, and someone else can win the side pot. Or another player can win both pots. But the all-in player can't win any of the later bets.

That's the negative side of table stakes. You can't buy more chips and raise if you smack a monster hand. So it's always a good idea to have an ample supply of chips sitting in front of you.

The Casino's Cut

The casino doesn't earn money when a player loses as it does in blackjack or roulette. Instead, the casino charges a fee for providing the venue. It collects this fee in one of three ways.

RAKE: A percent of the pot is set aside by the dealer before the chips are passed to the winner. It's usually five or ten percent, and there is a dollar-limit cap on the amount. Three or four dollars is common, so a $50 pot might have the same rake as a pot twice that size. It depends on the game.

TIME CHARGE: The dealer collects a fee from every player on the half hour.

BUTTON CHARGE: The dealer collects a fee from every player on the button.

One system isn't necessarily "better" but you'll notice that a rake favors **tight**, or conservative, players who maximize profit on fewer hands; it's better to win a couple of large pots rather than many small ones. In contrast, a time charge or button charge tends to penalize patience in the short run, and it encourages **loose** players who are willing to gamble on speculative hands.

Then again, loose players are exactly the kind of opponents you want to encourage.

Whatever method the casino uses, it adds up. A typical hour of poker will cost a player $10 to $20 depending on the game. An afternoon or evening of poker can easily put $50 to $100 into the casino's coffers. So you might finish a session ahead by

$200 when you actually won $300. Or you might go home poorer by $75 when you actually won $25.

In other words, being an average player will cost you money. The only way to consistently win at poker and beat the rake or collection is by being much better than average.

Toking the Dealer

A **toke** is a tip in casino-industry parlance. Casino dealers typically earn half or more of their money from tokes. For example, dealers at MGM Grand in Las Vegas had a total average income of $63,728 and a base pay of $5.35 per hour in 2000. The difference was tokes. And remember, MGM is the largest hotel property in North America (5,005 rooms). Dealers at smaller casinos earn much less.

Most people toke when they win a pot, usually fifty cents or $1. Some people toke when the dealer gives them change. It doesn't require an elaborate ritual; just toss the dealer a chip and say, "This is for you."

In Review

A♥ **It's your responsibility to protect your hand** and prevent it from being fouled. One way to do this is to put a short stack of chips on your cards to prevent them from being accidentally mucked by the dealer.

2♥ **Don't muck your hand in a showdown** unless you're absolutely certain that it's a loser. The rule is that the cards speak; don't rely on verbal declarations.

3♥ **Poker rules prohibit** splashing, string bets, and acting out of turn.

4♥ **Buying chips** during a hand is not allowed. You can only play with table stakes, the chips you have available.

5♥ **Casinos earn a profit** with poker by raking the pot (taking a portion of each pot), collecting a fee per seat at timed intervals, or collecting a fee on the button.

6♥ **Tokes** (tips) are the major source of a dealer's income. It's customary to tip fifty cents or $1 when you win a pot.

Part 2

Strategies for Hold 'Em

Chapter 4

Starting Hands and Position

REMEMBER THE LOTTERY EXAMPLE BACK IN CHAPTER 1? YOU could buy the first two numbers of a lottery ticket for a penny. Would you continue with that ticket if the numbers were duds? No, you'd throw it away and start fresh.

The same principle applies to hold 'em starting cards.

Dancing With Them That Brung Ya

The title of this section comes from an old Texas saying that is frequently used these days in the world of politics. "Dancing with them that brung ya" means that you're entirely dependent upon whomever or whatever brought you to "the party." You cannot dance with others because your fortune is tied to the fate of your partners or benefactors.

Starting cards are your dance partners in the world of poker.

Low-quality starting cards are bad dancers that will often embarrass you at the shindig. They're unreliable and they frequently fail at the most critical moment.

In contrast, high-quality starting cards generally perform well, and they consistently earn more than they cost.

A Good Starting Hand Has...

Starting hands are like everything else in poker, very situational. Your position in relation to the button, the number of active players, the number of bets or raises ahead of you, and the possibility of bets or raises behind you all have an enormous impact on the viability of any particular combination of cards.

So the "good" attributes listed on the next few pages are only the first standards for judging a hand. In other words, a hand with some good qualities is not necessarily always playable. More importantly, any hand that doesn't meet these basic standards can be immediately folded.

A note about notation:

• Lowercase "s" after a card combination (AKs, T9s, etc.) indicates the cards are of the same suit.

• Lowercase "n" after a card combination (QJn, 98n, etc.) indicates the cards are not of the same suit.

• Card combinations without "s" or "n" can be either suited or not suited.

• "T" stands for ten.

First we'll cover desirable hand attributes, and then we'll group the hands into ranks of relative value.

BIG CARDS

Let's say you hold AK and your opponent holds 87 before the flop. It's a curious truth that you both have an exactly equal chance of finishing the hand with a pair, two pairs, trips, a full house, or **quads** (four of a kind). But in a **heads-up** situation (only these two hands in competition) AK has a tremendous advantage because it will win if 87 does not improve to at least a pair. And AK will win if both hands improve equally. Consider a board showing the following:

AK was beating 87 before the flop, after the flop, and throughout the rest of the hand. Both players finished with a full house, but AK finished with jacks full of aces, while 87 dragged in with jacks full of eights.

So, **big cards** are good. Two cards that are jacks or higher always deserve a second look (though they're not necessarily always playable).

SUITED CARDS

Two cards of the same suit flop a four-card flush about eleven percent of the time. When that happens, the probability of finishing with a flush is better than one-in-three (2:1). **Suited cards** always deserve a second look, but only long enough to determine if they have additional good attributes. Suit alone is not enough to play a starting hand.

CONNECTORS

Cards that are next to each other in rank have a higher probability of making a straight. This probability drops dramatically as the gap between the cards increases. JT can make a straight four ways (AKQ, KQ9, Q98, 987) while J7 can only make a straight with T98. As with suited cards, **connectors** by themselves are not good enough to play a starting hand, but it's an attribute you should consider.

PAIRS

A **pocket pair** is generally a good thing. Of course AA is worth considerably more than 22, but any pair should get a second look.

Pairs are typically divided into three groups that reflect their relative power and profitability. Big pairs are AA through JJ. Medium pairs are TT through 77. Small pairs are 66 and below.

A WORD ABOUT TENS

Tens are a strange breed in the hold 'em world. They're not really big cards, but they can often carry a hand like big cards. For example, TT is closer in strength to JJ than to 99. And a ten is required for any high straight, so JT is often as powerful at QJ. Tens can be valuable, but they should be played carefully, especially when they're in gapped hands.

Ranking the Starting Hands

The following ranks are general, and there is a range of value within each rank. Keep in mind that things usually change on the flop. Nevertheless, a premium hand like AA will consistently

Hold 'Em Starting Hands

Premium hands	AA, KK, QQ, JJ, AK
Average hands	AQ, AJ, KQ, KJ, QJ, JT, AT, TT, 99, 88
Bargain hands	T9s and suited connectors down to 54s
	77 and pairs below
	Axs (suited hands containing an ace and any small card)
	KTs, QTs, J9s
Trash	Any hand that doesn't appear in the above three groups

Hands without "s" or "n" indicate both suited and non-suited.

earn more money than a bargain hand like 76s. Also remember that the suited version of a hand is always much stronger than the mixed-suit version.

HEADS UP COMPARISONS

Premium hands are the most reliable and profitable combinations. Big pairs can frequently pick up the pot without improvement, and a single ace or king on the board will often put AK over the top.

In contrast, average hands are generally less reliable and less profitable. They usually need improvement, and they're frequently beaten by premium hands.

Bargain hands continue the downward trend in quality. They almost always need improvement, and they sometimes lose even when the board gives them a boost. Nevertheless, they're still profitable when played carefully.

Trash hands fall right off the scale of profitability. They almost always cost money over the long-term regardless of how well they are played. One example would be 76n. That combination would be buried against premium and average hands like KK, AQ, and KJ if the flop were unexceptional (QT7 or JT4).

Note that some poker authors divide hold 'em starting hands into as many as eight categories plus trash. This is because there is a big difference between a nearly premium combination like AQs and something much closer to the bargain end like ATn. While this distinction is very important, I decided not to cross your eyes with a list that has multiple categories and six-dozen entries. Clearly, AJs is superior to JTn, KQs is stronger than QJn, and AA has an advantage over AKn. The more you play hold 'em, the more you'll learn the subtle nuances of these combinations, and you'll see that every hand really deserves its own category (see Chapter 6).

BIG PAIRS AND POETIC JUSTICE

Poker has many similarities to the game of life, and the relative strength of big pairs is one example. Big pairs push other hands around. They dominate the game like behemoths. But big pairs have a fatal weakness. They don't perform as well when there are many players in the pot. The probability of someone hitting a long-shot hand goes up; so it's like the little guys piling on to defeat the bully. In contrast, average hands and bargain hands that are suited and connectors tend to play very well against multiple competitors. These hands win less frequently, but when they hit it's often a doozy.

Smarter Bet Tip
Some hands are "borderline trash" like K9s, Q9s, J8s, and T9n. It's not necessarily always incorrect to play them, and you'll sometimes see an expert throw in borderline hands to mix up opponents, but it's a judgment call. These hands are frequently more trouble than they're worth. Beginners should avoid them.

TEMPTING TRASH

You'll frequently see people winning with Kx, Qx, 92s, 65n, and other garbage. If you play hold 'em for any length of time (especially at lower limits), you'll occasionally be beaten silly by these hands. Here's a typical scenario. You hold A♠ K♠ and your opponent has 6♣ 5♥. The board shows:

You flopped a four-flush and top pair. The turn improved you to two pairs, but your opponent played trash. She went for a **gut-shot straight draw** (needed one specific rank), and she made it on the river. Ouch! It happens.

Losing a pile o' chips can seriously mess with your attitude and put you **on tilt**. You may be tempted to play loose and crazy like the person who beat you. Don't do it!

Remember, any two cards *can* win. But trash probably won't.

Position is Power

Now that you know more about starting hands, let's go back to the round I described in Chapter 2. You'll recall that I said Kenny played his hand poorly. Here are all the hands:

Seat 1 Kenny: 7♣ 6♣ Called $3
Seat 2 Larry: A♦ K♦ Raised $6

Seat 3 Felecia: J♠ J♥ Raised $9

Seat 4-6: T♣ 2♠, 8♠ 4♣, K♥ 2♣ Folded

Seat 7 (button): 9♥ 5♥ Folded

Seat 8 Tom (little blind): Q♥ J♣ Folded

Seat 9 Jane (big blind): A♣ A♠ Raised $12

Kenny folded after Jane capped the pot. He lost $3 without seeing the flop.

Let's take Kenny out of seat 1 and put him on the button (last to act before the blinds). How would he play 76s facing two raises? Do you think Kenny would muck his cards and save some money? Yes, he probably would.

Okay, let's put Kenny back into seat 1, and swap Jane (AA) with Felecia (JJ). Jane makes the second raise behind Larry (AK). What would Felecia do? Would she be thinking about the cards Larry and Jane are holding? Yes, Felecia would see two strong raisers and correctly suspect that at least one of them might have a pair that would beat her two jacks. She would probably call rather than raise.

The lesson here is that position is power. The later you act, the more information you have about your opponents. In fact, all hold 'em strategy varies in direct relation to a player's position (it's like the Theory of Relativity applied to poker).

Early position is generally defined as the first three seats to act. **Middle position** would be the next two (or three) seats, and **late position** would be the final three.

Premium hands can be played in any position, but they're particularly well suited for raising in early position.

Average hands also can be played in any position if the game conditions are right. That's a big "if" that we'll cover later, but average hands are generally best suited to middle position and late position in a pot that hasn't been too aggressively raised.

Bargain hands are best suited for late position in an unraised pot. This insures that a bargain hand will get enough action to be profitable if the flop is a good one.

We'll expand the previous three paragraphs into a detailed pre-flop strategy in Chapter 6, but first we're going to cover poker economics and the general effects of folding, calling, and raising.

In the meantime, just remember that Kenny was foolish to play a bargain hand in early position. His call and fold exposed him as an inept player. Larry and Jane saw that immediately and both made a mental note to use the information later in the game.

In Review

♠A **The best hold 'em starting hands** include big cards, suited cards, connectors, or pairs. It usually takes two or three of these attributes to make a playable starting hand.

♦2 **Trash hands** may sometimes look tempting, but they invariably cost more than they win.

♦3 **Position is power** in hold 'em. Players who are closer to the button have more information about their opponents.

♦4 **Some starting hands** are most profitable in early position, and some are best played in late position.

Chapter 5

5 ♥

Poker Economics

"I HAVE EXACTLY SEVEN CARDS. I CAN'T DRAW MORE, AND MY opponents can see most of my hand. The only real decisions are bet, raise, or fold. Where's the control? Where's the strategy?"

That's what people who are familiar with blackjack and video poker often say when they first encounter hold 'em or seven-card stud.

The traditional concept of strategy as something to "use" on the implements of the game (the cards) works well in some contests, but genuine poker is more Zen-like. Poker strategy is about having a superior understanding of the relative strength of hands in their current and possibly future form. This knowledge allows you to compete when you have an advantage, and it gives you the ability to disappear like a ninja when an opponent is poised to strike. It's martial arts with cards. Your power is exercised through the outwardly simple tools of checking or betting, and folding, calling, or raising.

The Power of Folding

Imagine if you sat in a 3-6 hold 'em game for four hours, and you did nothing but fold. Not counting your seat fees, you'd lose about $15 per hour in blind bets or $60 during the session.

That's roughly comparable to what Larry won on just one pot (in our Chapter 2 example).

Now imagine if you played like Kenny and called every hand. That would cost about $80 per hour or $320 during a session, and that's just one call and no raises before the flop. The cost increases with every raise and every round. Kenny has to win a lot more chips to cover the price of not folding.

Muhammad Ali said, "Float like a butterfly, and sting like a bee." The poker equivalent of this philosophy is **tight and aggressive**. Your opponents should be swinging at air most of the time. Remember, every player has an equal probability of being dealt the best hand. The only way to create a favorable imbalance is to spend nothing or very little on losing hands, and cause your opponents to contribute a lot when a hand is a winner.

So folding has more power than most people realize. Let's say your opponent has the strongest possible hand, a royal flush.

What happens when you fold? Your opponent's royal flush loses some of its value. If everyone folds then a royal flush is essentially worthless.

Fortunately for us, most players don't fold or they fold later than they should, and thus it is the weaker hands that give the stronger ones value.

Only about 20% of hold 'em starting hands are playable, and a win rate of 30% to 60% is common with even the strongest starters (depending on the game). That means you should be folding about 80% of your hands before the flop, and about half of the rest should be folded after the flop or on the turn. Only about 10% of your starting hands will generate 100% of your winnings in a typical game. Of course, some nights will be hotter than others, and good hands sometimes come in streaks, but profitable poker involves a lot of waiting and constant trash removal.

You'll find this approach will differ greatly from the approach taken by most players, especially at the lower limits, where calling a blind bet is almost as automatic as an ante.

Pot Odds and Betting Decisions

Here's a quick quiz. You hold JT in late position and the flop comes Q84 **rainbow** (mixed suits). That gives you a gutshot draw to a straight. Should you call a bet on the flop or fold?

The answer is that you don't have enough information to make that decision. I haven't told you how much money is in the pot or the size of the bet. Those two figures are used to calculate **pot odds**, a system that helps you decide if a hand is worth pursuing.

Essentially, it's a refined version of saying, "Hey, this bet is too expensive." Or in some circumstances, "What a bargain!"

The calculation is simple. A player compares the money in the pot to the proposed bet. For example, $24 in the pot and $4 to call means the pot is six times larger than the bet. The pot odds are 6:1 (or some people say the pot is "offering" 6:1).

Sounds great, but what's the chance of actually winning that money? If the odds against the hand (essentially the probability of losing) are worse than 6:1, the hand should be folded. Why? Because in the long run the hand will not earn enough to justify the cost of the competition.

Let's say the pot odds are 6:1 and the odds against the hand are 11:1. For simplicity we'll make these dollars. The player will win $6 once and lose $1 eleven times. The deficit is $5. Not good. Roulette would be a cheaper game.

But if the pot odds are larger, 11:1 pot odds and only 6:1 against the hand, the player will win $11 once and lose $1 six times. That's a positive gain of $5. The hand should be played.

Of course, there's no way to predict exactly when that one win will occur, but it doesn't matter. It's a like owning a slot machine. The individual spins aren't as important as the long-term favorable odds.

POT ODDS MADE EASY

But how can you know the exact odds against a hand? In most cases you can't know exactly, but you can estimate very easily. Here's a classic example. You hold:

and the board shows:

This is a no-brainer. You have fifteen **outs** (cards in the deck that will complete the hand). Eight cards in the deck will give you a straight, and nine cards will give you a flush. Two of those cards are the same (giving you a straight flush), so the total is fifteen rather than seventeen.

A four-card flush always has nine outs. An open-ended four-card straight (four adjacent ranks) has eight outs. Gutshot straights have four outs. Two pairs to a full house is four outs. Pairs to trips is two outs.

The next two tables give you the probability and odds against improving on the flop and after the flop.

One easy way to calculate the probability of improving without memorizing the table is to simply multiply the outs by 4,

Probability of Improving on the Flop

Hand	Improvement	Probability	Odds Against
Any two cards	Making a pair	32.4%	2:1
Suited	Four-flush	10.9%	8:1
Pocket pair	Trips	11.8%	7.5:1

Probability of Improving After the Flop

Outs	Probability	Odds	Outs	Probability	Odds
1	4.3%	22.5:1	9	35%	2:1
2	8.4%	11:1	10	38.4%	1.5:1
3	12.5%	7:1	11	41.7	1.5:1
4	16.5%	5:1	12	45%	1.25:1
5	20.4%	4:1	13	48.1	1:1
6	24.1%	3:1	14	51.2	1:1
7	27.8%	2.5:1	15	54.1	1:1
8	31.5%	2:1	16	57.0	0.75:1

Odds against are rounded. Probability of improving after the flop is with two cards to come (turn and river).

and then put a percent sign behind it. That will get you close to the real number.

Another way is to just learn the odds for the most common hands. An open-ended draw to a straight flush is better than 1:1. Four-card straights and four-card flushes are about 2:1. Two pairs to a full house is 5:1, and one pair to trips is 11:1 (after the flop).

Okay, let's consider the hand in the most recent example, Q♥ J♥ with a board of A♣ T♥ 9♥. The pot holds $56 and the price of a call is $4. Is this a good bet?

Yes, it is. The pot is offering a hefty 14:1, and odds of making a straight or flush are about 1:1. You have a tremendous edge. This hand is worth a raise (but we'll get to raises in a later section).

POT ODDS MADE EVEN EASIER

Here's a way to make pot odds even easier to calculate (in case you really hate math). You don't have to know the exact amount of money in the pot. Just guess. Look in the center of the table and make a reasonable estimate, then compare it to the bet you're considering. Those are the pot odds.

Now, let's go back to the original question of the inside straight. You hold JT in late position and the flop comes Q84 rainbow. The pot has $30 and it will cost $8 to call a raise. What should you do?

The pot is offering less than 4:1; the odds against the straight are 5:1. This is a hand you should toss.

But what if the pot has $68 and the cost of a call is only $4? Then you're correct in calling on the flop and perhaps also on the turn if a nine does not appear (depending on the board).

As a general rule, big pots make it easy for **drawing hands** (hands that need improvement) to justify sticking around. Smaller pots aren't worth the risk. Think about how that affects the big pairs vs. bargain hands effect that I described in the previous chapter. An enormous pot with a cheap price for entry is not what a big pair wants to see. In fact, some very unlikely hands can become playable if the pot odds are large enough.

IMPLIED POT ODDS

Let's say you're on the button with 66. Four players call ahead of you. The pot is offering 5.5:1 (including the blinds). The chance of flopping trips is 7.5:1. This would seem to indicate a fold, but remember that you'll likely win bets in later rounds if you flop a six. The value of those extra expected bets should be included when you decide to call or fold before the flop.

In other words, the value of the pot at any given moment should be only part of the calculation. You should also reasonably estimate the value of the bets that will come when you hit a hand. Conversely, if hitting a hand will still leave you vulnerable, or your opponents will fold because the board will be exceptionally scary, then the **implied odds** are considerably less or perhaps even reversed.

Smarter Bet Tip

Drawing to a four-flush or an open-ended four-card straight generally requires a large pot and at least two opponents (preferably more than two) on the flop and turn because the odds against making the hand are 2:1. One win must exceed the price of two losses for the play to be profitable.

Calling vs. Raising

Moe is a friend of mine and a great guy, but he's a really bad poker player. No matter how much advice I give him, he has no patience for the intricacies of the game. Moe once complained, "Everyone always folds when I raise with a good hand."

It never occurred to him that raising isn't just a way to build the pot; it's also a powerful tool for changing the pot odds, thus making some hands unprofitable to play. Moe doesn't want to think about pot odds because he says, "It hurts my head." He just wants to win hands.

LOOSE AND PASSIVE

Poor Moe. He wins plenty of hands, but his pots are usually small. Moe is **loose** (frequently willing to put money in the pot), and he's **passive** (only bets and raises with extremely strong hands). In Moe's mind this "conservative" approach saves money when hands go bad; the savings supposedly allow him to play more hands and win more pots. But this thinking is all wrong. Loose and passive is a style of play that builds pots for other people. A guy like Moe is a **calling station**, the type of player who will call to "keep you honest" even when you're obviously holding a superior hand. Moe is an ideal opponent. He's the poker equivalent of an ATM.

LOOSE AND AGGRESSIVE

Jay will sometimes raise without even looking at his cards. Yes, some people actually do this. I suppose they think it's exciting. This style of play is loose and **aggressive**. Players like Jay are very dangerous because they're difficult to read. Jay might raise with trash or with a premium hand. Who knows? He's not stupid, but he's reckless. Jay will…not…fold unless he's absolutely sure that he's beaten, and he'll enthusiastically build a pot while hoping to catch a miracle. Sometimes it happens; a lot of time it doesn't. Jay's not a long-term winner, but he tends to magnify the money shifts at a table, and he alters pot odds in ways that are not always beneficial to **advantage players**. Going heads up with Jay can be profitable, but he's not an ideal opponent.

TIGHT AND PASSIVE

Mickey is the exact opposite of Jay. He doesn't play a lot of hands, and he rarely raises. He's the sort of person who disappears when Jay comes charging into a pot. Players like Mickey are **tight** and passive. They're sometimes called **rocks**. Mickey doesn't lose a lot, and he doesn't win a lot. He's very predictable, very beatable, but not a source of big profit for advantage players.

TIGHT AND AGGRESSIVE

Larry, Jane, and Felecia are all tight and aggressive. They're nearly as unpredictable and dangerous as Jay when they're in a hand because they frequently raise rather than just call. But they're also like Mickey, difficult to pin down. They check when opponents expect them to bet, and they fold when others are hoping for a call or raise.

There is no way to absolutely predict what a tight and aggressive player will do because the cards, the pot, and the other players are creating a per-hand strategy that is constantly adjusting to the immediate situation. Tight and aggressive players can be a lot of fun to watch, but a real challenge to beat.

IT ALL DEPENDS

Betting or raising can have a variety of effects depending on the situation. Raising with a premium hand is generally correct, but not always. Raising with an apparently marginal hand isn't necessarily wrong (especially if your opponent is Mickey). Everything is situational. The math always works, but it works differently as the mix of opponents changes.

This is an important concept. Keep it in mind as we cover the betting and raising strategies in the next chapter.

In Review

A♥ **Folding** is a powerful strategy for minimizing losses. Only about 20% of hold 'em starting hands are playable, and a win rate of 30% to 60% is common for even the strongest starters (depending on the game).

2♥ **Pot odds** is a system of comparing the potential profit of a bet to the possibility of winning a hand. When the profit is higher than the risk, the hand should be played.

3♥ **Big pots** with a cheap price for entry are good value for drawing hands, and they're dangerous for big pairs.

4♥ **Raising** is a powerful tool for manipulating pot odds and the size of the pot.

5♥ **Loose and passive** players tend to lose money. Players generally become more profitable as they become tighter and more aggressive.

Chapter 6

6
♦

Before the Flop

IF ALL PLAYERS WERE EXTREME VERSIONS OF MOE, EVERYONE would call your bets and nobody would raise. If they were all radical versions of Mickey, you could raise with trash under the gun and consistently **steal the blinds** because everyone (including the blinds) would fold thinking that you had AA. In fact, an average table has a mixture of players, and they're not always absolutely one way or another. We'll cover table selection in Chapter 9, but it's important to note here that poker strategy adjusts to accommodate the mood of the table. Your decisions should reflect the actions taken by particular opponents. A raise from Jay is entirely different than a raise from Mickey. And of course position (yours and theirs) plays an important role in your evaluation.

Opponents and Overall Strategy

For convenience, let's call a table "typical low-limit" if it has a mix of opponents and leans to the loose side. Most of the players are live ones or **weak** (tend to play poorly), a couple are solid, and perhaps one is a tight/aggressive expert who is killing time while waiting for a seat in a 20-40 game. Three or more callers (usually more) stick around for the flop.

The betting limits of our typical game are between 2-4 and 6-12, inclusive. Above 6-12 the players tend to tighten considerably. For example, a raise under the gun, or a raise in late position with no early callers, has a reasonable chance of stealing the blinds in a 20-40 game. That rarely happens when the limits are 2-4.

The strategies presented here are valid for any betting limit or mix of opponents, but the examples and exceptions focus primarily on low-limit contests.

MORE FOLD 'EM THAN HOLD 'EM

You can expect to see about thirty hands per hour if the table is full and the dealers are reasonably competent. If you only play premium, average, and occasionally bargain hands, that will be about 20% of all the hands you'll be dealt, or about six playable hands per hour. Two or maybe three of those hands will be winners. Think about that. Six or seven pots in a session will usually be your entire profit. The size of those pots and your chance of winning them are directly affected by the way you play before the flop.

GENERAL GOALS BEFORE THE FLOP

Premium hands want few opponents, a large pot, and a high price for entry (thus discouraging bargain hands). Premium hands create this condition by raising and limiting the field.

Bargain hands want to cheaply see the flop, so they **limp in** without a raise when possible. Conversely, if a bargain hand is in late position with a lot of callers, then it sometimes raises for value (doubles the size of the pot while getting excellent pot odds), or it might try to steal the blinds.

Average hands tend to play like premium hands in early position, and more like bargain hands in later position.

Early Position

This is the pre-flop strategy for early position. Note that the term "raised pot" refers to action from a seat on your right. Raises from behind are covered later.

EP Premium hands and an unraised pot: Raise with all premium hands in early position.

EP Premium hands and a raised pot: Reraise AA, KK, QQ, and JJ. Just call with AK. Cap the pot with AA, KK, or QQ if someone raises behind you, but evaluate your opponent and slow down with JJ; you may be up against a better pair. You should definitely reraise with AKs if a raise comes from behind and four or more players are in the hand, but with three or less just call any raise.

Keep in mind that AKs is a drawing hand; much of its value comes from the contributions of multiple opponents.

EP Average hands and an unraised pot: Raise with AQ, AJ, KQs, and TT. Call with the rest of the suited average hands, KQn, 99, and 88. Throw away everything else.

EP Average hands and a raised pot: Reraise AQs and TT. Call AJs and KQs. Fold everything else unless the raiser is loose and tends to raise with substandard hands. If he is, and if you reasonably expect many callers (four or more), then call with all the suited average hands, AQn, 99, and 88. Toss the rest of the unsuited hands.

EP Bargain hands and an unraised pot: Throw them all away unless the game is extremely and consistently loose/passive and you are certain to get many callers and no raises. If these perfect conditions exist, you can sometimes limp in. Remember, Kenny was in early position when he tried to limp in with low suited connectors, and he was buried by three raisers. So don't say I didn't warn you.

If the game is tight, and your opponents are experienced, you should occasionally raise with a bargain hand in early position just to throw the watchers off. But most of your opponents in low-limit games won't be experienced. They'll be clueless and entirely unresponsive to nuance plays. Don't waste your time or your chips.

EP Bargain hands and a raised pot: Throw them all away.

EP Two raises: If you're in the third seat and facing two raises, fold everything except premium hands. Follow the strategy for premium hands and a raised pot.

Middle Position

MP Premium hands: Same strategy as in early position.

MP Average hands and an unraised pot: Raise everything except QJ and JT; call with those.

MP Average hands and a raised pot: Reraise AQs and TT. Call with the suited hands and pairs. If the raiser is loose and tends to overvalue his starting hands, also call with AQn, AJn, and KQn. Throw away the rest of the unsuited combinations.

MP Bargain hands: Same strategy as in early position.

MP Two raises or a capped pot: Play only premium hands and sometimes TT if both raisers are loose and reckless. Follow premium strategy with one exception. If it's three bets to you, don't cap the pot every time. Instead, just call about half the time and give the original raiser a chance to cap the pot. This will disguise your hand and give you information about the original raiser. If she caps, then she probably has a premium hand. If she only calls, then she's probably holding a higher-quality average hand.

Hold 'Em Starting Hands

Premium hands	AA, KK, QQ, JJ, AK
Average hands	AQ, AJ, KQ, KJ, QJ, JT, AT, TT, 99, 88
Bargain hands	T9s and suited connectors down to 54s
	77 and pairs below
	Axs (suited hands containing an ace and any small card)
	KTs, QTs, J9s
Trash	Any hand that doesn't appear in the above three groups

Note that this table is identical to the one in Chapter 4. It's repeated here so you don't have to flip back and forth between chapters.

Late Position

LP Premium hands: Same strategy as in early and middle position.

LP Average hands and an unraised pot: Same strategy as in middle position except also raise QJs and JTs if there are four or more callers ahead of you.

LP Average hands and a raised pot: Same strategy as in middle position.

LP Bargain hands and an unraised pot: Fold all the bargain hands except pairs if there are three or fewer callers. Stay in if there are four or more callers. If you're on the button with a lot of callers (only one or two people have folded), occasionally raise with the bargain hands.

Conversely, if the game is tight and you're in late position with no callers, raise with a bargain hand in an attempt to steal the blinds.

LP Bargain hands and a raised pot: Fold everything unless nearly everyone is in the pot, the game is extremely loose, your opponents are weak, and you're on the button. Then call carefully with the bargain hands (see the tip on page 90).

LP Two raises or a capped pot: Same strategy as in middle position except if there are many callers (nearly the whole table). Then you can also play AQs, AJs, and KQs.

The Blinds

Remember that the blinds are last to act before the flop and first to act in all the later rounds. Also keep in mind that the big blind has already bet, so the only decision here is to raise or call a raise.

Generally you should play the blinds with a late-position strategy, but occasionally you can play a bit looser if there was an early raiser and a lot of callers because you might be looking at a huge pile o' chips and a single extra bet as the price for entry. Pot odds might be 10:1 or better. If that's the case, go ahead and call a raise with all the average hands, bargain hands, and even some marginal trash like Kxs and T8s.

If you have a bargain hand or marginal trash (Qxs, Txs, 89n, Axn, and similar combinations) in the little blind with a lot of callers and no raises, call for one-half bet or less. If there has been a raise, follow late-position strategy.

The issue of **defending the blind** against a possible steal is a complex subset of poker strategy. You won't have to face this much in loose games because opportunities to steal are rare. If there are other callers, simply fold when your hand doesn't warrant a call. If you're heads up against a late raiser, fold the first time it happens and raise the second time (with a bargain hand or better).

A Raise From Behind

If you play a starting hand correctly, then it's always worth a call and possibly a reraise when a raise comes from behind. Pot odds will help you make this decision.

What if you incorrectly play a hand and find yourself trapped holding a bargain combination while facing two or three opponents and a raise? Just fold. Learn from the mistake and don't do that again. Recognize that the table is tighter and more aggressive than you thought. You'll need to tighten up, too. Jettison the bargain hands in middle position. Jettison the unsuited average hands.

Exceptions, Exceptions

The more you learn about hold 'em, the more you'll find exceptions to the pre-flop strategy I have outlined. There are situations when it is correct to raise with trash, and there are times when a premium hand clearly does not merit a raise.

There are plenty of experts who would not raise TT in early position, and some who would raise 99. Other disputed hands include AT, A9, JT, and 88. In fact, every hand has its exceptions.

The lesson here is that you shouldn't play like an automaton. Instead, you should consider position, the pot, and your opponents, then choose the best strategy for that particular situation. In most cases you'll find the best strategy is the one outlined on the previous pages.

Smarter Bet Tip
Calling a raise is safer when your action will end the round. That's not necessarily the same as being on the button. A late raiser to your right and active players to your left expose you to a possible raising war.

In Review

A♦ **Only about 20% of hold 'em starting hands
are playable,** and 10% or less go on to become winners.
So it's important to quickly identify those hands and play
them for maximum profit.

2♦ **Most hands are unplayable in early position.**
The range of hands that are playable increases when a
seat is closer to the button.

3♦ **Premium hands want few opponents and a
large pot.** Bargain hands want to cheaply see the flop,
so they limp in without a raise when possible. Average
hands tend to play like premium hands in early position,
and more like bargain hands in later position.

4♦ **If you come across a situation that has you
completely stumped,** follow this advice: When in doubt,
throw it out.

Chapter 7

| 7 |
| ♥ |

The Flop and Beyond

THE FLOP IS THE PIVOTAL MOMENT IN HOLD 'EM. FIVE OF THE seven cards (71%) have been revealed. The character of the hand is generally set, and three rounds of betting are ahead. The flop is the best time to drop an obvious loser or begin the process of pumping a hopeful winner.

The Good, the Bad, and the Vulnerable

Poker hands generally fall into one of the following categories during the last three rounds of hold 'em.

Strong hand: A combination that is the nuts or unlikely to be beaten.

Vulnerable leading hand: A hand that is definitely leading, but could easily become a second-best hand in a later round. Trips is a typical example of a vulnerable leading hand.

Weak leading hand: This hand is probably leading but extremely vulnerable. There are a lot of ways it could lose. One example would be AQ with a flop of QJ8. If AQ was the only pre-flop raiser, then it's probably top pair (though it's entirely possible someone else is holding QJ for two pairs, or T9 for a straight). Either way, the hand is vulnerable to anyone holding a nine or ten, especially JT, AT, J9, QT, and Q9. There might even be an 88 lurking out there.

Second-best hand: Using the previous example, someone holding AJ would be second best to AQ. AQ would be second best to QJ. Players who are second best and don't realize it are the primary source of profit in poker.

Drawing hand: This is typically a four-card flush or four-card straight looking for a fifth card, but it also includes any hand that is clearly an underdog and hoping to improve. One example would be two pairs drawing to a full house when the board and pattern of betting indicate that someone has a flush.

Obvious loser: A hand like 7♥ 6♥ against a board like Q♠ Q♣ J♠ with a raise and reraise ahead is an obvious loser. Hands competing with the nuts or in other unwinnable situations are said to be **drawing dead**.

Smarter Bet Factoid

The relative value of a starting hand often shifts dramatically on the flop. Hands that seemed anemic may be suddenly strong, and a strong starter such as AKs may become almost worthless. A sudden shift doesn't necessarily mean that a pre-flop raise was incorrect, but the flop does create a new situation that you should recognize.

Strong hands want to extract the maximum amount of money from the table. It's a pleasant job, but not as easy as you might imagine because experienced opponents can often tell when someone is holding a better combination, and they drop.

Drawing hands generally want to continue as cheaply as possible, though they sometimes want to build the pot if the pot odds will exceed the probability of hitting their hand.

Vulnerable and weak leading hands want to make each round as expensive as possible so that drawing hands won't stick around and improve.

Second-best hands can improve and win, but they often don't, so they want to see the turn and river very cheaply or for free, otherwise they're looking to fold.

Obvious losers want to quickly identify their unhappy condition and stop putting money in the pot.

Reading the Flop

Position plays an important role on the flop (as it does in every round of hold 'em). A bet, raise, and reraise tells you a lot, as does a bet and long line of callers. It also helps to remember how an opponent played pre-flop. Here are a few examples:

This is a flop that looks good to AA, KK, and QQ (assuming they're not all simultaneously competing). Of course, this is a strong flop for JJ, and it also looks inviting to AJ, KJ, QJ, and JT. See how the latter hands can be crushed by the former? All of them are vulnerable to T9 and 65. How can you tell who has what? Let's say that you're holding AJ and you were the only raiser before the flop. It's likely that your pair of jacks with an ace kicker is the best hand. But if you called a pre-flop raise, AJ is possibly second best (behind a higher pocket pair). This is nearly certain if that same player raises again.

This is the kind of flop that usually gets a lot of action and breaks a lot of bankrolls. KK is probably the best hand here if there was a lot of pre-flop raising. If there wasn't, then someone may have limped in with AT or T9. Any of these three hands will hurt AA, QQ, JJ, AK, AQ, AJ, KQ, QJ, or KJ unless a ten falls and makes a straight for anyone holding an ace. Another diamond may finish a flush. If the board pairs then the straight or flush may be beaten by a full house. One way or another it's going to be a monster pot with a wild finish.

This flop is often bad news for AJn, KJn, JJ, and TT. Anyone holding a queen is in good shape unless another heart falls to make a flush, or another low card appears to fill in a straight.

Flops like this usually produce small pots because hands without an ace are unlikely to stick around if anyone bets. AK is a strong favorite over other hands that have an ace and a lower kicker. A5 has a full house but may still be beaten by a higher full house if the wrong card comes on the turn or the river. It happens.

This is a scary flop for Ad Ah. There are a lot of ways to lose, including to a straight, a flush on the turn or river, or two pairs. Note that high cards next to each other in rank or one-gapped often give opponents two pairs.

This is the kind of flop you'll love when holding 88, 99, or TT (as well as higher pairs). It's death to big unpaired cards.

There are countless more examples, but these few flops give you a taste of the thought process and the dynamics of hold 'em at this stage. The best way to handle these situations is largely determined by your position and the actions of your opponents.

Bet or Check, Raise or Fold

Strategy on the flop and afterwards is much more complex and situational than pre-flop strategy. That's because there are only 1,326 possible two-card starting hands but over 2.5 million five-card combinations. Nevertheless, hands of a certain type generally can be played similarly.

TWO OVERCARDS

If you've got no pair but two strong **overcards** with a non-threatening board (example: AK with a flop of T62 rainbow), it's

Smarter Bet Tip

Middle or bottom pair is significantly weaker than top pair and it's often unplayable unless you have a strong kicker and the opposition is clearly weak. Example: You hold **AT** and the flop is **JT6**. You bet in early position and get only two callers. It's probable that you're up against a ten with a lower kicker or opponents drawing to straights.

usually a good idea to come out betting if nobody has yet entered the pot. Everyone may fold to you. If not, then you'll at least thin the field. A raise from behind will alert you to the fact that somebody has a pair or better. Go ahead and call one raise. Don't call any reraises. If someone bets ahead of you, evaluate the flop and then fold if the pot is not large enough. Beware of suited cards, straight cards, high connectors, or high pairs on the board. Yes, it's tough to part with AK and other big connectors, but calling with less than a pair in this situation would be a waste of money.

TOP PAIR, TWO PAIRS, AND TRIPS

If you've got top pair with a strong kicker, two pairs, or trips, then come out betting on the flop. Raise if someone bets ahead of you. Opponents calling behind you rather than raising would generally indicate that you're probably the best hand (unless you're up against a monster combination that is waiting for the next round).

But what if someone raises you?

A SHORT COURSE IN POKER ESP

You've been raised on the flop. What is the opponent raising with? Think back to the way she played her hand before the flop. You can usually **put an opponent on a hand** (accurately read what she's holding) by matching the board to pre-flop and post-flop betting. Here's an example.

Let's say you hold AQ in early position. You put in the only raise before the flop. Five players call. The flop comes Q72 rainbow. You bet on the flop and are raised. What is the raiser holding?

Think about it. It's unlikely that she's holding Q7 or 72 unless she's someone who calls pre-flop raises with complete trash. Also, she didn't reraise you before the flop. That would mean she's probably not holding a big pair. Instead, it's likely that she's holding KQ, QJ, QT (which you can beat), or perhaps 77 or 22 (which would beat you). How do you narrow the guess? Reraise her. She'll probably just call with big cards, but she'll likely raise you back (cap) with a set.

Smarter Bet Tip
You'll have a strong urge to check and call rather than bet or raise when a hand is less than perfect. Resist that urge unless a check and call are clearly the correct strategy. If a bet or raise is incorrect, then folding is usually a better option than calling.

Remember that the cost of a raise here is only half the cost of a bet in a later round, so it's well worth the price if it exposes her hand. Of course, there's a possibility that she might **slow-play** trips (call rather than cap on the flop and raise you later on the turn). That's fine with you because you won't be calling any raises on the turn unless your hand improves.

Whatever she does on the flop, you should stick around for the turn. Bet if the turn-card is a **blank** (doesn't clearly help anyone) or if you improve. Another raise from her on the turn makes it almost certain that she's holding a set (or has improved to two pairs). You're beaten and can drop. Yes, you lost some chips, but these things happen.

On the other hand, a call from her on the turn rather than a raise means she's probably second-best and hanging on. Why doesn't she raise on the turn to bluff you? Remember, she doesn't know what you're holding. It might be QQ. Everything you've done (raise, bet, reraise, bet) has been consistent with holding a big pocket pair. Only a psychic or a maniac would raise with a mediocre hand in this situation.

SECOND-BEST

Let's say you're on the opposite side of the previous example holding QJ and looking at a flop of Q72 rainbow. You dutifully raised on the flop (as I recommended) and you were reraised. Guess what? You gained some valuable information that will save you money on the turn. You're probably up against AA, KK, QQ, AQ, or KQ. A call here would be correct. The turn will either improve your hand and give you a reason to continue, or a blank will give you a reason to fold if someone bets into you. Just drop the hand.

STRAIGHT OR BETTER

Flopping a nut-straight, nut-flush, or better isn't too common. Hands like this should be slow-played on the flop. Checking and calling will lure people into hanging around for the turn and double bets. That's when you should become aggressive. On the other hand, don't slow-play without the nuts. Be especially careful with low cards (example: 87 with JT9).

DRAWING HANDS

Are you drawing to a strong hand? If yes, then check if you're in early position, and call or raise on the flop if the pot odds justify it (they usually do in loose games). If you're drawing to a strong hand and you also have top pair, just play it aggressively.

OBVIOUS LOSERS

Check and fold if the flop misses you completely and you don't have two overcards. Fold if you've got middle or bottom pair with a weak kicker (example: 98 and AQ9). Fold if you have top pair with a weak kicker, and you're facing a raise (example: A5 and AQJ). Fold when you're clearly second best unless you have a draw to the best hand and favorable pot odds. Generally, if a hand is not worth a bet or raise, then it's not worth a call (except when drawing to the nuts or near-nuts).

EXCEPTIONS, EXCEPTIONS

Sometimes you can read the table perfectly and win with middle or bottom pair. Sometimes you can miss the flop completely and finish with trips on the river. Sometimes it is correct to **chase** with a second-best hand. Poker has millions of "sometimes" situations. As I mentioned in Chapter 6, you should not play like an automaton, but the strategies here are optimal in the majority of circumstances.

Later Rounds

The noose tightens on the turn. Bets double, and the probability of improving drops dramatically. Fold here if your opponent is leading, knows that she's leading, and you don't have a clear idea how you will win. Remember, bankrolls are mostly consumed by too much calling on the flop and turn, not by bad beats on the river.

The correct long-term strategy is usually to call or raise pre-flop with a strong or promising hand, evaluate the flop and get out if a hand isn't probably best or drawing to be best. We'll cover more betting strategies and subjects like bluffing in Chapter 9, but first, let's take a look at some other poker versions.

In Review

A♥ **The flop is the pivotal moment** in hold 'em. Five of the seven cards (71%) have been revealed. Hands at this stage generally fall into four categories: strong hands, vulnerable hands, drawing hands, and losers.

2♥ **Opponents' betting patterns** on the flop and before the flop can often give you a good idea of what they're holding.

3♥ **Generally, strong hands should be slow-played** until the turn. Vulnerable hands should be aggressively played. Drawing hands should be played in ways that maximize their value when they hit. Losers should be dropped.

Part 3

3 ♠

Other Games, Other Strategies

Chapter 8

8 ♦

Seven-Card Stud and Other Games

NEW POKER VERSIONS ARE EASY TO LEARN WHEN YOU UNDER-
stand the basics of pot odds, the power of folding, the
importance of selecting the best starting hands, and the
other concepts we've covered in the previous chapters.

Of course, specific strategies change with each version
(sometimes dramatically), but remember that the underly-
ing systems remain the same. A raise is still a tool for getting opponents to drop. Weak hands should be protected.
Drawing hands should be played cheaply, etc.

Seven-Card Stud

Seven-card stud doesn't use community cards like hold 'em. Each player builds a poker hand from seven personal cards, four of which are exposed.

The game begins with an ante. Each player receives two cards face down and one face up. The player with the lowest exposed card is required to make a small initial bet (less than the table minimum) called a **bring-in**.

The player to the left of the bring-in can call the bet to the table minimum, raise, or fold. Action proceeds clockwise from that position. This round is called **third street**. Subsequent rounds are similarly named for the number of cards in a hand, though **seventh street** is sometimes called the river.

Action on fourth street and later rounds begins with the player who has the highest exposed hand. Fourth street through sixth street are dealt face up and seventh street is dealt face down. Bets double on fifth street.

Smarter Bet Factoid

Suit is used to determine the bring-in when cards are of the same rank. The suits are valued lowest to highest in alphabetical order: clubs, diamonds, hearts, spades.

THE IMPORTANCE OF LIVE CARDS

Most of the strategy of seven-card stud revolves around the concept of live cards. Let's say you're dealt a starting hand of:

The jack is the **door card** (exposed card). You look out on the table and see that four of your six opponents are showing hearts. That means the probability of finishing with a heart flush has dropped dramatically. If the other two opponents show queens or higher then your hand is nearly worthless. Conversely, no hearts and a lot of small cards showing would justify a call if the pot has not been too aggressively raised. If you do choose to proceed, then you must note when a competitor receives a card that you were wanting, and you must remember the cards that are folded. Let's say another jack arrives on fourth street. It's worth less if two jacks have already gone into the muck.

SEVEN-CARD STUD STARTING HANDS

As you might expect, suited cards, pairs, trips, and connectors make the most powerful starting hands. While I don't want to imply any exact parallels with hold 'em starting hands, it's fair to say that that the same general patterns apply. You should play big pairs hard and fast. Drawing hands should be played cheaply or raised for value when the pot odds exceed the probability of hitting the hand.

Trips should be slow-played on third street, and then raised on fourth or fifth street depending on how many players are still in the hand and the degree of strength they're showing.

If you don't have any of the above and no big cards, then fold the hand. Keep in mind that there are two betting rounds before you see five cards compared to one in hold 'em, and about 39% of seven-card combinations finish with two pairs or better. So highly speculative hands are simply not economical unless the table is extremely passive.

Smarter Bet Tip

Beware of paired door cards in opponents' hands. This dramatically increases the probability that you're up against trips (or better), particularly when the door card is of a higher rank.

LATER STREETS

Five of the seven cards (71% of the hand) have been revealed by fifth street. This is where bets double, so it's best to fold here if you're not leading and you don't have a strong draw. Remember that the overall probability of seeing any particular seven-card combination is exactly the same in seven-card stud as in hold 'em, but the extra variable is live cards. So use the charts from Chapter 5 and subtract outs when you see them in other hands.

Omaha Hi/Lo

The original version of this game is called Omaha. It's hold 'em played with four cards in the pocket, and exactly two of those four cards must be used to make a hand. So if you have:

and the board shows:

You don't have a straight or a flush. You have a pair of aces. The best five-card Omaha hand from the above seven cards is A♣ A♥ K♣ 9♣ 7♠ (using two of the four cards in your hand).

These days Omaha is usually played as Omaha hi/lo. The high hand splits the pot with the lowest hand that is eight or better (which really means eight-high or worse). The low hand in the previous example is A♥ 3♥ 4♥ 5♣ 6♣. Straights and flushes don't count when competing for the lowest hand, so the best combination is ace through five. For more on low hands, see the section on razz.

OMAHA HI/LO STARTING HANDS

Omaha hi/lo is a volatile contest because so many cards are in play and there are so many ways to win. Pots often become very large because everyone figures they have a shot. A lone pair of jacks or queens can often win an entire pot in hold 'em, but this rarely happens in Omaha hi/lo. If an ace and king hit the board, it's nearly certain that someone is holding at least one of those cards, probably both. High pairs and even two pairs are anemic hands. A typical winner is a straight or better, and remember, half the pot goes to a low hand.

The best starting hands are combinations that can work for both high and low. Examples would be A♠ A♦ 2♦ 3♠, A♥ K♦ 3♦ 4♥, or A♣ 2♣ K♥ K♦. A playable, but less flexible hand would be A♠ K♠ Q♥ Q♣ because this could only capture high. Examples of hands to toss include Q♦ J♥ 7♠ 6♠ and K♦ J♠ 10♥ 9♥. Note that these hands could be played as two-card combinations in hold 'em, but they simply won't hold up in Omaha hi/lo.

Other Games

Pineapple is hold 'em played with three pocket cards. One of the three must be discarded on the flop. The rest of the game plays like hold 'em.

Razz is seven-card stud played for low. The rules are identical to regular seven-card stud except the hand ranks are reversed. Pairs and above are bad (straights and flushes don't count). The best hand is ace through five which is called a **wheel** or **bicycle**. The next-best hand is A-2-3-4-6, third-best is A-2-3-5-6, and so on. A hand like 2-3-4-5-8 is much worse, and anything above ten is generally unplayable. The way to win at razz is to start with three low cards (A-2-3 is best), and keep track of how many lows are still alive as the hand develops. Seven-card stud can also be played hi/lo.

Lowball is five-card draw played for low. See the razz section for more on ranking low hands.

Five-card draw is the original poker version. The game uses an ante, and a rotating dealer. Five cards are dealt face down. Action begins to the left of the dealer. Players have an opportunity to discard and receive replacement cards after the first round of betting. There is another betting round followed by a showdown.

In Review

♦A There are no community cards in seven-card stud. A player receives seven personal cards. Three are dealt face down and four are face up. Action begins with the lowest exposed card on the first round. Action on later rounds begins with the highest exposed hand.

♦2 Omaha is similar to hold 'em except it is played with four cards in the pocket. Exactly two of those cards must be used to make a poker hand. In the hi/lo version of Omaha, the pot is split between the player holding the high hand and the player holding the low hand (when the low hand is eight or "better").

♦3 It's easy for beginners to be confused about what beats what when playing razz or lowball. The solution is to determine the highest hand as you would normally, then flip the decision. Thus 2-4-5-7-8 would lose to 2-3-5-7-9 when playing for high, but it would win when playing for low because nine is higher than eight.

Chapter 9

$$\boxed{\begin{array}{c} 9 \\ \heartsuit \end{array}}$$

Advanced Strategies

THE FOLLOWING STRATEGIES APPLY TO ALL FORMS OF POKER, but for consistency I will use examples from hold 'em.

Raising to Get a Free Card

A **free card** is a powerful multi-layer strategy that is generally unknown among casual poker players. Here's how it works.

You're in late position. Four people call ahead of you before the flop and you raise with A♣ T♣. All four players and the big blind call your raise. The flop produces J♣ 10♦ 2♣. Four players check and the fifth bets. What should you do?

You should raise. You may have the best hand right now, but even if you don't, a raise will make you look as if you do. You have a 1 in 2 chance of making the nut flush, and your opponents will remember that you also raised before the flop. Why is this memory important?

If the turn fails to help anyone, your opponents may check to you because they'll want to avoid another raise. They'll expect you to bet, but you won't bet. You'll check and end the round. They'll be relieved, but it's you who has reason to celebrate. You've just given yourself a **free card**. It's an extra opportunity to improve your hand without investing anything in the process.

Conversely, you don't want to give away free cards. There's not much you can do when an expert **semi-bluffs** like this. But most opponents aren't experts. Generally, you should bet the flop and the turn when your hand is leading. Make opponents pay to see the cards.

Also on the subject of raising, don't be put off if you find yourself in a casino that has spread-limit games (typical in Las Vegas). Use your knowledge of pot odds and limp in with a minimum bet when a hand is speculative. Build the pot with a medium-sized bet if you're holding the nuts, or raise the maximum when holding a vulnerable hand (thus making a c all unprofitable for your opponents). Ironically, beginners often do it the other way; they bet modestly with vulnerable hands and blow it out with monsters. Big mistake.

Betting or Calling on the End

Smarter Bet Factoid

Even bad players get good hands from time to time. Opponents who raise on the turn are rarely bluffing. Those who bet or raise on the river are (almost) never bluffing.

Folding on the end is rarely correct unless you're absolutely certain that a hand is a loser. Pot odds are usually so enormous by this point that any reasonable chance for a win deserves a call. That's why Jane called on the end in the Chapter 2 example. Of course, if a hand is clearly busted, then you should save yourself the bet.

Conversely, it's rarely correct to bet on the end unless the bet is a pure bluff, or your hand is exceptionally strong. That's because (as I explained in the previous paragraph) good players will call you only if they might win. That's not a problem when you're holding the nuts or something close, but it's a big problem when the lead is not so well defined. You might be holding a big pair of aces and find yourself beaten by two pairs. Checking in this situation would save money (that's what Jane did, and she saved herself the cost of a reraise). Remember, betting on the end is pointless if only the losers fold.

Bluffing

You may have noticed that I barely use the word "bluff" in this book. That's because good players don't bluff a lot. Instead they semi-bluff, raise for value, and make other strategic bets that confuse their opponents.

Pure deception is like pepper. You should use it sparingly. The complexity of your basic game should be the major source of misdirection. Besides, everyone has seen the movies, and they imagine themselves capable of exposing a bluff.

I once had an opponent who decided I was a loose bluffer when he saw me (correctly) fold a number of hands that had originally merited raises. The next time I raised, he reraised, and I crushed him with a full house. So your best opportunity for profit is not in bluffing. Instead, profit comes when you capitalize on the mistakes of others.

Also remember that it's nearly impossible to "pure" bluff multiple opponents when you're holding trash. Somebody is going to have a hand that is worth a call.

CHECK-RAISE AND OTHER DECEPTIONS

A check-raise is an aggressive move. It's the poker equivalent of giving opponents a "wedgie" because you're trapping them for two bets rather than one, thus nuking their pot odds. Of course, you must be certain that someone will bet after you check. If nobody does, then the table gets a free card. You've been semi-bluffed!

Table Selection

You'll learn a lot about poker if you play only with people who have superior skills. But you'll go broke paying for that education. So you should avoid sitting with more than two or three good players. Ideally, the majority of your opponents should be loose/passive. Practically, you'll also see a fair number of over-the-top loose/aggressive players at the lower limits. You won't regularly run into tight/passive until you get into games above 6-12, but loose/passive players sometimes temporarily morph into conservative players if they have a good run of cards.

Give a table about thirty minutes, and if four or more of your opponents are playing well, cash in and find greener pastures. Remember that winning pots and playing well are not necessarily synonymous. As I said in Chapter 1, there is lucky, and there is good. Luck eventually turns. Good is forever.

Tells

Tells are behaviors that give you a clue about what an opponent is holding. There are dozens of tells, but they're not always reliable because a player may not correctly value his cards. In any case, here are some of the strongest tells.

Shaking hands: Players with shaking hands believe they are on the verge of winning. Be careful.

Long pause and then a call: You've just seen someone with a drawing hand trying to calculate pot odds.

Sighs and rolling eyes: This is usually bad acting to cover a strong hand (unless the player folds).

Looking away: Once again, this is an attempt to conceal sheer glee. Beware.

Looking at you: A player who looks at you (rather than through you) is interested in your reaction because he has a vulnerable hand. Note that this doesn't necessarily mean that your hand is stronger.

The World of Poker

Poker is a journey of learning; no player can ever reach a final state of absolute expertise because poker has infinite complexity and nuances. Part of the learning experience is simply playing. Another part is something that experts refer to as "thinking about the game when you're away from the game." This is how true poker skill is developed. It starts with reading books like this and continues with conversations and contacts with other players.

Here are some resources to help you on the journey.

Poker Digest: This magazine is published by the same company that publishes *Casino Player* (the number one casino gaming magazine in the world). *Poker Digest* is usually available free at card rooms, and it's also sold by subscription. The magazine has in-depth articles and interviews on every conceivable aspect of the poker experience. www.pokerdigest.com

Card Player: Another excellent poker magazine available by subscription and also free in most card rooms. www.cardplayer.com

Wilson Software: There are a lot of computer poker simulations out there, but Wilson's Turbo series is consistently ranked highest by poker professionals. Each game version has dozens of cyber-opponents that play realistically at different levels of expertise, or you can create your own custom opponents. The high-speed test and reporting options are awesome. Wilson software isn't cheap, but it's worth every penny. www.wilsonsw.com

SmarterBet.com: This is a site dedicated to all of the Smarter Bet Guides. Here you'll find essays on poker strategy, information about other gambling games, and you can drop me an e-mail and ask me questions. www.smarterbet.com

POKER TOURNAMENTS

Poker tournaments are an excellent way to play a lot of poker while simultaneously limiting your exposure. There are hundreds of tournaments around the country, and most have entry fees in the range of $25-$100. A portion of the fee pays for the venue and the rest goes into a prize pool that is won by the top ten or so players (depending on the size of the tournament). And of course, some tournaments are played for big money. There are more than two dozen major events in North America. *Poker Digest* has all the info.

Welcome to the world of poker!

In Review

A♥ **Never give a free card** when your hand is leading and vulnerable. Take a free card whenever possible if your hand is second-best and hoping to improve.

2♥ **Calling on the end** is usually correct unless your hand is an obvious loser.

3♥ **Checking on the end** is best when your hand is leading but vulnerable.

4♥ **Bluffing is a tactic** that should be used sparingly. The complexity of your basic game should be the major source of misdirection.

5♥ **Table selection** is an important part of profitable poker. You should quit a table if four or more opponents are playing better than you.

Glossary

action (1) Dollars wagered; more dollars is synonymous with more action. (2) A player's turn to act.

all in Betting all of one's chips.

ante A mandatory first bet in seven-card stud and five-card draw.

bad beat An improbable loss.

big cards Face cards and aces.

blank A card that has no effect on a hand; it does not help or hurt.

blind bet A mandatory bet in flop games. Typically, the two players to the left of the designated dealer post blind bets.

board The poker table.

bring-in A mandatory first-round opening bet in seven-card stud. The bring-in is made by the player with the lowest exposed card.

burn To remove a card from the top of the deck without putting it into play. Burning one or more cards is a procedure to discourage cheating.

button Also known as a puck or a buck. A button is a marker that identifies the designated dealer in flop games. The button moves one player to the left after each hand.

calling station A player who calls too much.

cap A limit to the number of raises in a round.

cards speak A poker rule that requires winners be determined by the cards and not by verbal declarations.

chase To call with a second-best hand.

check To offer no bet in a round that does not have a mandatory bet. A player who checks must call, raise, or fold if another player bets.

check-raise To check and later raise an opponent's wager in the same round.

community cards Cards that are dealt face-up and shared by all the players in a hand.

connectors Two cards of adjacent rank.

count down The process of counting the money in a pot to determine if everyone has contributed the proper amount.

dead cards See live cards.

designated dealer A rotating designation used to determine blind bets and the order of betting in Texas hold 'em and other flop games.

door card The first exposed card in a seven-card stud hand.

drawing dead Playing a hand that cannot win.

drawing hand A hand that is hoping to improve.

fixed-limit A poker game in which the bet limits are fixed at specific levels.

flop The second round of betting in Texas hold 'em and other flop games.

flop games Poker versions with five community cards and four rounds of betting.

foul To cause a poker hand to be invalid.

free card A card that comes "free" because there was no betting in the previous round.

gutshot straight draw A draw to an inside straight (needing exactly one rank rather than one of two).

heads up Two players who compete when everyone else has folded.

hole cards The first two cards that are dealt face down in Texas hold 'em or seven-card stud.

kicker The highest unpaired card in a poker hand when that hand is not a straight or flush.

limp in To call rather than raise the big blind.

live cards Any cards that have not yet been exposed in seven-card stud.

live one A weak player.

loose A player who is likely to bet or call rather than fold.

muck To throw away cards. Also, the area where cards are discarded.

no-limit A poker game in which there are no restrictions on the amount that can be bet.

nuts Cards that make an unbeatable hand.

on tilt A bad mood that adversely affects judgment and causes a person to play badly or erratically.

one player to a hand A poker rule that requires each player to make decisions alone and without consultation.

outs Cards that will improve a hand.

overcard In flop games, a personal card that has a higher rank than the cards on the board.

pocket cards See hole cards.

pocket rockets Two aces in the pocket.

post To place a bet (typically refers to a blind bet).

pot odds The size of the pot compared to the size of the proposed bet. This is expressed as a ratio.

pot-limit A poker game in which any amount can be bet up to the amount in the pot.

protect your hand To handle cards in way that reduces the possibility of the hand being fouled.

put an opponent on a hand An accurate guess of what an opponent is holding.

quad Four-of-a-kind.

rainbow Three or four cards that are not of the same suit.

rake Money collected by a casino as a percentage of the pot or as a flat fee.

river The final round of betting in Texas hold 'em or seven card stud.

rock An extremely conservative player.

semi-bluff Betting or raising with a weak hand when there is a good possibility it could improve.

set Three-of-a-kind made with a pocket pair.

show one, show all A poker rule that allows everyone at the table to see a player's hand if one opponent sees that hand.

showdown The end of the last round of betting in a poker hand when all remaining players reveal their cards.

side pot An extra pot that is created from bets made after a player goes all in to the main pot.

slow-play To play a strong hand passively, representing it as weak in order to draw players into the pot.

splashing the pot To throw chips into the center of the table rather than putting them in front of one's position.

spread-limit A poker game in which there is a fixed minimum and maximum bet, but a player can wager any amount between those two figures.

steal the blinds Raising before the flop with a sub-standard hand in an attempt to get the blinds to fold.

string bet or string raise To call a bet, and then raise after assessing an opponent's reaction. Not allowed in most poker games.

table stakes A poker rule that requires all players to wager with only the chips that are on the table at the beginning of the hand.

tell Unconscious movements or body positions that indicate what a player is holding.

tight A player who is averse to taking risks.

time A verbal request for a pause in the game.

toke Casino industry jargon for a tip (gratuity).

trips Three-of-a-kind.

turn The third round of betting (fourth community card) in flop games.

under the gun The first player to act in a flop game.

Index

Numbers followed by *f* and *t* indicate figures and tables.

About the Author

Basil Nestor is an author, journalist, columnist for *Casino Player* magazine, and creator of *CompuServe's* advice-series *Ask the Gambling Expert*.

He began his career as an editor for affiliates of CBS and NBC. As a freelance television producer he authored pieces for CNN, PBS, and other networks. Basil's career as a journalist merged with his gaming expertise when he created the award-winning documentary *Casinos in the Community*, an in-depth report on the gaming industry in Atlantic City. He also produced *Riverboat*, a television program that reveals how gaming is changing the Midwest. His subsequent work has involved numerous casino companies including *Players Casinos* (*now Harrah's*) and *Resorts International*.

Basil's extensive studies of gambling strategies and game theory, his research into the history of gaming, and his personal experiences at the tables provide the backdrop for his writing. It's a body of work that has informed and entertained millions of people.

He has authored six books (including *the Unofficial Guide to Casino Gambling*) and dozens of articles for *Casino Player CompuServe's Las Vegas Forum*.

Got a gambling question? Visit *SmarterBet.com* and send Basil an e-mail.